The Status of
the Arab Woman

The Status of the Arab Woman

A SELECT BIBLIOGRAPHY

COMPILED BY
Samira Rafidi Meghdessian
UNDER THE AUSPICES OF
the Institute for Women's Studies
in the Arab World,
Beirut University College, Lebanon

Greenwood Press
Westport, Connecticut

ISBN 0 313 22548 6

First published in the United States in 1980 by
Greenwood Press, a division of Congressional Information
Service Incorporated, 88 Post Road West, Wesport,
Connecticut 06880

© Institute for Women's Studies in the Arab World, 1980

Library of Congress Cataloging in Publication Data

Meghdessian, Samira Rafidi
  The Status of the Arab woman.

Includes indexes.

1. WOMEN – ARAB Countries – BIBLIOGRAPHY. 2. WOMEN, MUSLIM –
BIBLIOGRAPHY. I. Title.
Z7964.A7M43 1980 [HQ1784]   016.3054′2′09174927
ISBN 0–313–22548–6 (llb. bdg.)   80–1028

Manufactured in Great Britain

Contents

Foreword by Rose Ghurayyib   7
Introduction   11
Bibliographies and Reference Works Consulted   17

The Bibliography   21
Cultural and Social Background of the Middle East   23
Conferences and Seminars on the Arab Woman   28
Women in Islam and the Law   32
Women in the Arab Middle East—General Works   50
Women in North Africa—General Works   83
Women in Individual Arab Countries   89
    Algeria   89
    Bahrain   97
    Egypt   98
    Iraq   111
    Jordan   113
    Kuwait   116
    Lebanon   118
    Libya   125
    Mauritania   126
    Morocco   127
    Oman   135
    Palestine   135
    Saudi Arabia   138
    Somalia   140
    Sudan   140
    Syria   145
    Tunisia   146

Contents

United Arab Emirates 156
Yemen 157

Author Index 159
Subject Index 173

Foreword

After a period of stagnation which lasted for over 500 years, the Arab countries emerged in the early part of the nineteenth century into an era of cultural awakening. This change was mainly induced by increased contact with the West through Napoleon Bonaparte's campaign in Egypt in 1798, and the efforts made by Muhammad Ali and his successors to introduce Western civilization into the lands they ruled or conquered. The second half of the nineteenth century witnessed the spread of modern schools in Egypt, Lebanon and Syria; the increased use of printing presses; the development of journalism; and the publication of old manuscripts. The same period saw the beginnings of the movement to translate Western science and literature into Arabic, as well as the introduction of Western arts such as drama, sculpture and music.

The emancipation of the Arab woman went hand-in-hand with a cultural revival which began to spread throughout the Arab regions soon to be known as the Middle East. Men and women writers contributed to create a feminist movement, campaigning against the veil, polygamy, unilateral divorce allowed to men, and other social forms of sexual discrimination. The last quarter of the nineteenth century saw the spread of women's education helped by the works of a group of women writers, poets and social leaders who directed charitable organizations and proclaimed social reform. In the first half of the twentieth century, other signs of female emancipation appeared. A large number of Arab women's journals were established. Women teachers, journalists, social workers, writers and poets multiplied. The higher professions were opened to women, and many women studied and practised medicine, pharmacy, dentistry, law and even engineering. Women gained the right to vote and be elected to parliament in Egypt, Iraq, Jordan, Lebanon, Syria and Tunisia.

However, in spite of the progress achieved in the fields of education and the professions, women leaders recognized that little success had been made in uprooting the traditional, stereotyped attitudes towards women and in eliminating the double standards for the two sexes which prevail to this day in Arab family life and society. The chief obstacle to reform lies in the stand taken by conservative and reactionary groups against any change in the old Koranic code of laws; it particularly applies to those laws pertaining to personal and family status which are generally unfair to women, thereby perpetuating the traditional concepts of women's cultural inferiority. This inequality is an issue that Furugh Hourani emphasized in her 1968 article on 'Uncertain Equality' in the London *Times* (see entry no. 477) where she stated that 'female education is more likely to affect change than legislation, and Arab women must be more active in demanding equality'. Another social obstacle to women's liberation that has been more recently understood is the wide divergence in educational levels among the Arab countries. Uniform progress is next to impossible since the less progressive countries continue to exert a retrogressive influence on the more progressive ones, and any change will necessitate serious efforts to improve the overall equality of education throughout the Middle East.

For the purpose of activating and improving the development of Arab women, the Institute for Women's Studies in the Arab World (IWSAW) was founded in 1973 at Beirut University College, Lebanon with a grant from the Ford Foundation. IWSAW is one of nine women's institutes established in nine Asian women's colleges that are joined together by the title of the Asian Women's Institute. The parent centre was founded in 1975, with its international office in Lucknow, India. The central objective which unites these sister institutions is 'to assist the women of Asia in their groping for self-fulfillment'.

The activities of IWSAW have concentrated on three areas of interest: research, documentation and communication. The following are some of the research projects that have been completed: 'A Study of the Works of Lebanese Women Artists' by Helen Khal (no. 1183); 'Concept of Women in Children's Textbooks' by Ilham Kallab (no. 1182); 'Adjustment of Women Students in an Arab College: Beirut University College' by Ghassan Rubeiz (no. 592); *A Survey of Rural Household Resource Allocation in Lebanon in 1975* by Dr. Joseph Phares, Father George di Napoli and Irene Lorfing (no. 1199); and 'May Ziadeh' by Rose Ghurayyib. Some of the research projects in progress are: 'Image and Status of Women in the Lebanese Press' by Richard Alouche (no. 1142); 'A Survey of the Development of Higher Education for Women in the Arab World' by Edith Hanania (no. 471); 'A Young Child Study' by Mary Makhouli and Julinda Abu Nasr; 'A Study of Contemporary Female Poets in the Arab World' in French by Rose Ghurayyib; 'The Effect of War on the Moral Development of Lebanese Children' by Julinda Abu Nasr, Sylvia Von Krieken, Irene Lorfing and Iman Khalifeh; and 'The Industrial Female Workers in Lebanon'. A bibliography on Arab women by Youssef Dagher (which will be in Arabic) is in preparation, while 'Arab Women in Population, Employment and Economic Development' (jointly prepared by IWSAW and ILO) is in the course of publication. Finally, IWSAW publishes a newsletter, *Al-Raida* (no. 489).

Rose Ghurayyib
Research Associate and Editor of *Al-Raida*,
Institute for Women's Studies in the Arab World

Introduction

SCOPE

This bibliography aims to provide a list of research material on the economic, legal, religious and social status of the Arab woman in the twentieth century. It is intended for the use of individual researchers, libraries, centres of Middle Eastern studies, and groups and research institutes concerned with the development of woman on an international level.

COVERAGE

The bibliography contains over 1,600 entries and includes all Arab countries from the Middle East and North Africa. It covers books, journal articles, conference proceedings, papers (published and unpublished), masters' theses, doctoral dissertations, and bibliographies (published separately or included in books). The great majority of the material has been published since 1950, but there is a certain amount of pre-1950 literature, which serves to provide an historical background. Most of the references are in English and French, but some appear in German, Italian and Spanish. The multilingual coverage is particularly apparent in the references on North Africa, where, of course, much of the research has been written in French; it also emphasizes the quantity of local material that has been included.

Specific attention has been given to the inclusion of works on subjects which have been avoided until very recently in traditional societies, such as female circumcision. Naturally, there is a great temptation to include general works on such subjects as family planning, family structure, society, child development and welfare that may relate to the Arab woman. Specific efforts have been made to include these works only when they deal with the Arab woman within the established framework of reference. Background material is listed in the sections on the 'Cultural and Social Background of the Middle East', 'Women in the Arab Middle East— General Works' and 'Women in North Africa—General Works'.

The section on the cultural and social background of the Middle East should in no way be considered as exhaustive. It is an attempt to provide a basic list of material on the subject and it is essential for researchers to make further consultation as follows:

a. Books dealing with Middle Eastern and North African society and its development. In recent years, the focus of interest on this area has resulted in valuable and up-to-date research. Most of the following books, for example, have chapters dealing with the Arab woman:

Anderson, J.N.D. *Islamic Law in Africa*. London: Frank Cass, 1978.

Clarke, J.I. and Fisher, W.B. *Populations of the Middle East and North Africa: a Geographical Approach*. New York: Holmes and Meier, 1972.

Cole, Donald Powell. *Nomads of the Nomads. The Āl-Murrah Bedouin of the Empty Quarter*. Illinois: AHM Publishing Corporation, 1975.

Costello, V.I. *Urbanization in the Middle East*. Cambridge: Cambridge University Press, 1977.

Halpern, Manfred. *Politics of Social Change in the Middle East and North Africa*. Princeton, N.J.: Princeton University Press, 1963.

Hazen, William and Mughisuddin, Mohammad. *Middle Eastern Subcultures: a Regional Approach*. Lexington, Mass.: Lexington Books, 1975.

Isenberg, Irwin. *The Arab World*. New York: H.W. Wilson, 1976.

Kennett, Austin. *Bedouin Justice, Law and Customs Among the Egyptian Bedouin*. London: Frank Cass, 1968.

Laffin, John. *The Arab Mind Considered, a Need for Understanding*. New York: Taplinger Publishing, 1975.

Mansfield, Peter. *The Arab World*. New York: T.Y. Crowell, 1976.

Mansfield, Peter. *The Arabs*. London: Penguin Books, 1979.

Milson, Menahem, ed. *Society and Political Structure in the Arab World*. New York: Humanities Press, 1973.

Pierce, Joe E. *Understanding the Middle East*. Rutland: C.E. Tuttle, 1971.

Pillai, K.C. *Light Through an Eastern Window*. New York: Robert Speller and Sons, 1977.

Savory, R.M., ed. *Introduction to Islamic Civilization*. London: Cambridge University Press, 1976.

b. Statistical yearbooks with education, working population, literacy and other demographic data. These are particularly important, since in some Arab countries population censuses have only recently been completed.

c. Basic Islamic and Christian texts such as the Koran and the Bible, and works interpreting them.

d. Statutes of individual countries, particularly sections dealing with family law (marriage, divorce, death) and civic rights (the vote, ownership, patrimony, etc.). These give a clear idea of the legal status of the Arab woman today.

ARRANGEMENT

The bibliography is arranged under general subjects and individual countries. Entries are numbered and arranged alphabetically by author as far as possible, regardless of form of material or language of publication, within each section. There is one exception in that the section on 'Conferences and Seminars on the Arab Woman' is arranged chronologically. However, individual papers presented at conferences and seminars are listed by author under the appropriate general subjects and individual countries. There are author and subject indexes, in which the numbers refer to entries and not to pages.

SOURCES

The collection at the Documentation Center at the Institute for Women's Studies in the Arab World (IWSAW) at Beirut University College, Lebanon has provided the basic core of this bibliography. Since its foundation in 1973, IWSAW has been conducting research into the Arab woman for the purposes of establishing a documentation centre. This research has centred around the following topics: status (economic, legal, religious and social); role (as daughter, sister, wife and mother); academic contributions; and relationship to society (family planning, birth control and other important social issues).

The list of references has been greatly enhanced by the efforts of several researchers (Dr. May Ahdeb-Yehia, Miss May Rihani, Dr. Audrey Gray, Dr. Julinda Abu Nasr, Mrs. Aileen Lee, Mrs. Mary Helen Kennedy, Miss Mona Barakat and Miss Najla Hussni) who collected material from the following sources:

Bibliothèque Orientale, St. Joseph University, Beirut, Lebanon.

Faculties of Economics and Social Sciences, St. Joseph University, Beirut, Lebanon.

Ford Foundation Library, Ford Foundation Office, Beirut, Lebanon.

Jafet Library, American University of Beirut, Beirut, Lebanon.

Middle East Social Sciences Index, Library of the American University of Cairo, Cairo, Egypt.

Near East School of Theology, Beirut, Lebanon.

Stoltzfus Library at the Beirut University College, Beirut, Lebanon.

Unesco Library, Unesco Headquarters, Paris, France.

United Nations, Economic Commission for Western Asia Documentation Center, Beirut, Lebanon.

A wealth of unpublished materials available from private collections and resulting from IWSAW's participation in various international conferences. These unpublished materials form an important feature of the bibliography.

In addition, a number of bibliographies and other reference works were consulted which in themselves led to further sources. These invaluable works appear in a separate list following this Introduction.

ACKNOWLEDGEMENTS

In compiling this bibliography I am indebted to the following: Dr. Julinda Abu Nasr, Director of IWSAW, for involvement in this project; Miss Mona Barakat and Miss Najla Hussni, research assistants at IWSAW, for their indefatigable verification of the sources and their valuable help in all the technical aspects of this work; Miss Nuha Azar, executive secretary at IWSAW, for typing the manuscript; and Dr. Guy David Nottingham, Visiting Professor of Communication Arts at Beirut University College, for assistance in the editing of the manuscript. I also wish to thank the Administration at Beirut University College for providing an environment conducive to individual research and development.

Samira Rafidi Meghdessian,
formerly Head Librarian, Beirut University College,
Institute for Women's Studies in the Arab World,
Beirut University College,
P.O. Box 11–4080,
Beirut,
Lebanon
November 1979

Bibliographies and Reference Works Consulted

Ahdab-Yehia, May and Rihani, May. 'A Bibliography of Recent Research on Family and Women in the Arab States.' Beirut: Institute for Women's Studies in the Arab World, Beirut University College, 1 June, 1976. (Mimeographed.)

Allman, J., Stone, J. and Ben Achour, Ch. 'A Bibliography of Recent Social Science Research on the Family in the Arab States.' Paris: Unesco Publications, Unesco Population Coordination Unit, Department of Social Sciences, 1974. (Mimeographed.)

American Council of Voluntary Agencies for Foreign Service. Technical Assistance Information Clearing House (TAICH). *Women: a Select, Annotated Bibliography of TAICH* Holdings. Part V. New York, 1975 and 1976.

Atiyeh, George N., comp. *The Contemporary Middle East, 1948-1973: a Selective and Annotated Bibliography.* Boston: G.K. Hall, 1975.

Birdsall, Nancy. *An Introduction to the Social Science Literature on 'Women's Place' and Fertility in the Developing World.* Annotated Bibliography, Vol. 2, No. 1. Washington, D.C.: Smithsonian Institution, 1973.

Boulding, Elise, Nuss, S.A., Carson, D.L. and Greenstein, M.A. *Handbook of International Data on Women.* New York: Halsted Press, John Wiley and Sons, 1976.

Buvinic, Mayra. *Women and World Development: an Anno-tated Bibliography Prepared under the Auspices of the American Association for the Advancement of Science.* Washington, D.C.: Overseas Development Council, 1976.

Canadian Newsletter of Research on Women, 1972– , three times a year, c/o Sociology Department, Ontario Institute for Studies on Education, 252 Bloor Street West, Toronto, Ontario.

Centre d'Études Pour le Monde Arabe Moderne (CEMAM) Reports. *Arab Culture and Society in Change: a Partially Annotated Bibliography.* Beirut: Dar ol-Mashreq and CEMAM, 1973.

Centre d'Études Pour le Monde Arabe Moderne (CEMAM) Reports, *Islamic Law and Change in Arab Society.* Beirut: Dar el-Mashreq and CEMAM, 1976.

Dagher, Joseph A. *L'Orient dans la litterature française d'après guerre, 1919–1933.* (Ouvrage subventionné par le gouvernement libanais.) Beirut: Edouard Angélil, 1937.

Doctoral Dissertations on the Middle East. London: University Microfilms International.

Fadil, Virginia. *A Selected Bibliography on Higher Education in the Middle East.* Carbondale, Ill.: Southern Illinois University, 1975.

Gray, Audrey Ward. *Childhood, Children and Child Rearing in the Arab Middle East: a Selected and Annotated Bibliography.* Beirut: Ford Foundation, March 1973.

Gulick, John and Gulick, Margaret E. *An Annotated Bibliography of Sources Concerned with Women in the Modern Muslim Middle East.* Princeton Near East Papers, No. 17. Princeton, N.J.: Princeton University Press, 1974.

ISIS: International Bulletin, 1976– , quarterly. ('ISIS is coordinating the International Feminist Network.') Isis Collective, Via della Pelliccia 31, 00153 Rome, Italy and Case Postale 301, 1227 Carouge/Geneva, Switzerland.

The Middle East Journal, 1947– , quarterly. (Contains a 'Bibliography of Periodical Literature'.) Washington, D.C.: The Middle East Institute.

O'Connor, Patricia. *Women: a Selected Bibliography.* Springfield, Ohio: Wittenberg University, 1973.

Pearson, J.D., comp. *Index Islamicus, 1906–55.* Cambridge: W. Heffer and Sons, 1958. (Reprinted in London: Mansell, 1972.)

Pearson, J.D., comp. *Index Islamicus, First Supplement, 1956–1960.* Cambridge: W. Heffer and Sons, 1962. (Reprinted in London: Mansell, 1973.)

Pearson, J.D., comp. *Index Islamicus, Second Supplement, 1961–1965.* Cambridge: W. Heffer and Sons, 1967. (Reprinted in London: Mansell, 1974.)

Pearson, J.D. and Walsh, Ann, comps. *Index Islamicus, Third Supplement, 1966–1970.* London: Mansell, 1972.

Pearson, J.D., comp. *Index Islamicus, Fourth Supplement, 1971–1975.* London: Mansell, 1977.

Al-Qazzaz, Ayad. *Women in the Arab World: an Annotated Bibliography.* Detroit, Mich.: Association of the Arab-American University Graduates, Aug. 1975.

Al-Qazzaz, Ayad. *Women in the Middle East and North Africa: an Annotated Bibliography.* Middle East Monographs, No. 2. Austin: University of Texas, 1977.

Rentz, Sophie Bassili, comp. *Directory of Social Scientists.* Cairo: American University of Cairo, Organization for the Promotion of Social Sciences in the Middle East, n.d.

Rihani, May. *Development as if Women Mattered: an Annotated Bibliography with a Third World Focus.* Occasional Paper, No. 10. Washington, D.C.: Overseas Development Council, 1978.

Selim, George Dimitri, comp. *American Doctoral Dissertations on the Arab World, 1883–1968*. Washington, D.C.: Library of Congress, 1970.

Selim, George Dimitri, comp. *American Doctoral Dissertations on the Arab World, 1883–1974*. 2nd edition. Washington, D.C.: Library of Congress, 1976.

Signs: Journal of Women in Culture and Society, 1975– , quarterly. Chicago: University of Chicago Press.

Tinker, Irene and Bo Bramsen, Michele, eds. *Women and World Development*. Washington, D.C.: American Association for the Advancement of Science and Overseas Development Council, 1976.

Women's International Network (WIN) News, 1975– , quarterly. Women's International Network, 187 Grant Street, Lexington, Mass. 02173.

Women in Pakistan and Other Islamic Countries: a Selected Bibliography with annotations (on Pakistan only). Karachi: Women's Resource Centre/Shirkat Gah, 1978.

Women Studies Abstracts, 1972– , quarterly. Rush, N.Y.: Rush Publishing.

Zuwiyya, Jalal, comp. *The Near East (South-West Asia and North Africa): a Bibliographic Study*. Metuchen, N.J.: Scarecrow Press, 1973.

The Bibliography

Cultural and Social Background
of the Middle East

1. Adams, Michael. *The Middle East: a Handbook*. New York: Praeger, 1971.
2. Antoun, Richard and Harik, Iliya, eds. *Rural Politics and Social Change in the Middle East*. Bloomington: Indiana University Press, 1972.
3. Antoun, Richard T. 'Social Organization and the Life Cycle in an Arab Village.' *Ethnology* 6 (1967): 294–308.
4. Asad, Talal. *The Kababish Arabs: Power, Authority and Consent in a Nomadic Tribe*. London: C. Hurst, 1970.
5. Baer, Gabriel. *Population and Society in the Arab East*. New York: Frederick A. Praeger, 1964.
6. Berger, Morroe. *The Arab World Today*. New York: Anchor Books—Doubleday, 1962.
7. Berger, Morroe. *The Middle Class in the Arab World*. (Privately printed for a Princeton University Conference, 1958.)
8. Berque, Jacques. *The Arabs: their History and Future*. London: Faber and Faber, 1964.
9. Burton, Richard F. *A Plain and Literal Translation of the Arabian Nights Entertainments, Entitled The Book of the Thousand Nights and a Night*; with introduction, explanatory note on the manners and customs of Moslem men, and a terminal essay upon the history of the nights, by Richard F. Burton. 10 Vols.

London: Burton Club for private subscribers only, 1886.

10. Burton, Richard F. *Supplemental Nights to the Book of the Thousand Nights and a Night*; with notes anthropological and explanatory by Richard F. Burton. 7 Vols. London: Burton Club for private subscribers only, 1886.

11. Charnay, Jean-Paul. *Islamic Culture and Socio-Economic Change*. Leiden: E.J. Brill, 1971.

12. Cogswell, Betty E. and Sussman, H.B., eds. *Cross-National Family Research*. Leiden: E.J. Brill, 1972.

13. Davis, J. *People of the Mediterranean: an Essay in Comparative Social Anthropology*. London: Routledge and Kegan Paul, 1977.

14. Dodd, Stuart Carter. *Social Relations in the Near East*. Beirut: American Press, 1940. (Reprinted in New York: AMS Press, 1975.)

15. 'The Evolution of the Moslem Family in the Middle Eastern Countries.' *International Social Science Bulletin* Part 4 (1953): 341–357.

16. Fisher, Sydney Nettleton. 'Social Forces in the Middle East.' Papers presented at a Conference sponsored by the Committee on the Near and Middle East of the Social Science Research Council, Ithaca, N.Y., Cornell University Press, 1955.

17. Gannagé, Pierre. 'L'évolution du droit de la famille au Proche-Orient et en Afrique de Nord.' *Travaux et Jours* no. 4 (Jan.–Feb. 1962): 53–68.

18. Gulick, John. *The Middle East: an Anthropological Perspective*. Pacific Palisades: Goodyear, 1976.

19. Hamady, Sania. *Temperament and Character of the Arabs*. New York: Twayne Publishers, 1960.

20. Hammond, Dorothy and Jablow, Alta. *Women: their Economic Role in Traditional Societies*. Reading, Mass.: Addison-Wesley, 1977.

21. Hammond, Dorothy and Jablow, Alta. *Women: their Familial Roles in Traditional Societies*. Reading, Mass.: Addison-Wesley, 1977.

22. Hammond, Dorothy and Jablow, Alta. *Women in*

Cultures of the World. Reading, Mass.: Addison-Wesley, 1976.

23. Hatab, Zuhair. Evolution of the Structures of the Arab Family. *Al-Raida* no. 6 (Nov. 1978): 8–9.

24. Holler, Joanne E. *Population Growth and Social Change in the Middle East.* Washington, D.C.: George Washington University, 1964.

25. 'Iz Istorii Emansipatsii Vostochnoi Zhenshchinui.' (De l'histoire de l'émancipation de la femme orientale.) *Novuy Vostok* 20–21 (1928): 406–416.

26. Izzeddin, Najla. *The Arab World.* Chicago: Henry Regnery, 1953.

27. Lane-Poole, Stanley, ed. *Arabian Society in the Middle Ages—Studies from the Thousand and One Nights by Edward William Lane.* London: Curzon Press, 1922. (New edn. 1971.)

28. Lerner, Daniel. *The Passing of Traditional Society: Modernizing the Middle East.* Glencoe, Ill.: Free Press, 1958.

29. Lutfiyya, A.M. and Churchill, C.W., eds. *Readings in Arab Middle Eastern Societies and Cultures.* The Hague: Mouton, 1970.

30. Macleod, R.B. 'The Arab Middle East: Some Social Psychological Problems.' *Journal of Social Issues* 15, 3 (1959): 69–75.

31. Marshall, John F. and Polgar, Steven. *Culture Natality, and Family Planning.* Carolina Monograph, no. 21. Chapel Hill: Carolina Population Center, 1975.

32. Nahas, M.K. 'The Family in the Arab World.' *Journal of Marriage and Family Living* 16, 4 (1954): 293–300.

33. Najarian, Pergouhi. 'Changing Patterns of Arab Family Life.' *Middle East Forum* (Jan. 1960): 11–17.

34. Nolte, Richard H. *The Modern Middle East.* New York: Atherton Press, 1963.

35. Patai, Raphael. *Golden River to Golden Road: Society, Culture and Change in the Middle East.* Philadelphia: University of Pennsylvania, 1962.

36. Patai, Raphael. *Sex and Family in the Bible and the Middle East.* New York: Doubleday, 1959.

37. Peristiany, J.G., ed. *Contributing to Mediterranean*

Sociology: Mediterranean Rural Communities and Social Change. The Hague: Mouton, 1968.

38. Peristiany, J.G., ed. *Honor and Shame: the Values of Mediterranean Society.* Chicago: University of Chicago Press, 1966.

39. Peristiany, J.G., ed. *Mediterranean Family Structures.* Cambridge: Cambridge University Press, 1976.

40. Polk, William and Chambers, R. *Beginnings of Modernization in the Middle East—the Nineteenth Century.* Chicago: University of Chicago Press, 1968.

41. Prothro, Edwin Terry and Diab, Lutfi. *Changing Family Patterns in the Arab East.* Syracuse: Syracuse University Press, 1974.

42. Prothro, Edwin Terry and Diab, Lutfi. *Evolution of the Muslim Family in the Arab East* (E/ECWA/POP/ WG. 12/BP.6). Beirut: Economic Commission for Western Asia, 1978.

43. Raphael, Dana, ed. *Being Female: Reproduction, Power and Change.* The Hague: Mouton, 1975.

44. Rivlin, Benjamin and Szyliowicz, J. *The Contemporary Middle East.* New York: Random House, 1965.

45. Rondot, Pierre. *The Changing Patterns of the Middle East.* London: Chatto and Windus, 1961.

46. Rosenfeld, Henry. 'Processes of Structural Change within the Arab Village Extended Family.' *American Anthropologist* 60 (1958): 1127–39.

47. Seklani, M., Rouissi, M. and Bchir, M. *Demography and Socio-Cultural Environment in the Arab Countries.* Beirut: UNICEF, Eastern Region, 1970.

48. Shiloh, Ailon. *Peoples and Cultures of the Middle East.* New York: Random House, 1969.

49. Sweet, Louise E. *Peoples and Cultures of the Middle East.* 2 Vols. New York: Natural History Press, 1970.

50. Szyliowicz, Joseph S. *Education and Modernization in the Middle East.* New York: Cornell University Press, 1973.

51. Talbi, Mohieddin. *Lexique sociologique des arabes: sexualité, parenté, groupe, antagonismes sociaux, richesse et pauvreté, gloire, qualifications morales.* Paris: Imprimerie de Carthage, 1967.

52. *Three Studies on National Integrations in the Arab World*. North Dartmouth, Mass.: Association of the Arab-American University Graduates, 1974.

53. Thornburg, Max Weston. *People and Policy in the Middle East: a Study of Social and Political Change as a Basis for United States Policy*. New York: Norton, 1964.

54. Al-Tikriti, Yunis H. 'Industrialization, Urbanization and Family Organization in the Middle East.' Ph.D. dissertation, University of Tennessee, 1967.

55. UNESCO Workshop on Family Adjustment to Social Change in the Middle East and North Africa. Beirut, July 1974.

56. United Nations. Economic Commission for Western Asia. 'Demographic and Related Socio-Economic Data Sheets for Countries of the Economic Commission for Western Asia, No. 2.' Beirut: ECWA, Jan. 1978.

57. Van Dervort, Thomas R. 'Social Dynamics and Political Change in the Middle East.' Ph.D. dissertation, University of Tennessee, 1967.

58. Van Nieuwenhuijze, C.A.O. *Social Stratification in the Middle East*. Leiden: E.J. Brill, 1965.

59. Van Nieuwenhuijze, C.A.O. *Sociology of the Middle East*. Leiden: E.J. Brill, 1971.

60. 'Visiting Patterns and Social Dynamics in Eastern Mediterranean Communities.' *Anthropological Quarterly* 47, 1 (Jan. 1953):n.p.

61. Zeltzer, Moshe. *Aspects of Near East Society*. New York: Bookman Associates, 1962.

Conferences and Seminars
on the Arab Woman

62. International Alliance of Women. Copenhagen, Denmark, 28 July–24 Aug., 1954.
63. United Nations. Seminar on the Status of Women in Family Law. Lomé, Togo, 18–31 Aug., 1964.
64. Fiftieth Anniversary Conference on the Population Crisis. Twentieth Century Challenge. Symposium on Birth Control and the Changing Status of Women. New York, 18–19 Oct., 1966.
65. American University of Beirut. Conference for Women. University Women in a Changing Society. Panel Discussion, 22 Apr., 1967.
66. Conference on Exploding Humanity. International Teach-In, Toronto University, Toronto, Nov., 1968.
67. UNESCO. Meeting of Experts on the Access of Girls and Women to Technical and Vocational Education in Arab Countries. Kuwait, 1–7 Nov., 1969.
68. International Women's Congress. Madrid, June 1970.
69. Regional Conference on Education, Vocational Training and Employment Opportunities for Girls and Women in African Countries. Rabat, Morocco, 20–29 May, 1971.
70. UNICEF, Arab League and Arab States Adult Functional Literacy Center. Seminar on Arab Women in National Development. Cairo, Egypt, 24–30 Sept., 1972.
71. Arab League. Family Committee. Resolutions of the First Seminar on the Arab Family. Kuwait, 18–21 Dec., 1972.

72. Middle East Studies Association. Seventh Annual Meeting, Milwaukee, Wis., 8–10 Nov., 1973.
73. American Anthropological Association. 72nd Annual Meeting, New Orleans, 28 Nov.–2 Dec., 1973.
74. Conférence sur la Condition de la Femme Libanaise et les Perspectives de sa Libération. Beirut, Lebanon, Dar el-Fan, 1974.
75. Eighth World Congress of Sociology. Toronto, 1974.
76. General Union of Yemeni Women. The First General Congress of Yemeni Women. Saium, Fifth Governorate, People's Democratic Republic of Yemen, 15–16 July, 1974.
77. General Union of Palestinian Women. Second Conference. Beirut, Lebanon, 5–10 Aug., 1974.
78. United Nations, FAO. Seminar on the Role of Women in Integrated Rural Development with Emphasis on Population Problems (FAO/UN/TF/75). Cairo, Egypt, 26 Oct.–3 Nov., 1974.
79. Colloquium on Women's Higher Education, New Challenges in a Changing Asia–Middle East. Memphis, Tenn., Oct. 1974.
79a. Middle East Studies Association. Eighth Annual Meeting, Boston, 6–9 Nov., 1974.
80. Seminar on Women and Social Development. Baghdad, Iraq, 28 Dec., 1975.
81. Afro-Asian Seminar on Women's Social Development. Alexandria, Egypt, Mar. 1975.
82. Seminar on Women in Development. Mexico City, Mexico, 16–18 June, 1975.
83. United Nations. World Conference. International Women's Year. Mexico City, Mexico, 19 June–2 July, 1975.
84. Conference on Population Policy from the Socio-Economic Perspective. Washington, D.C., Resources for the Future, 1975.
85. 8th Annual Convention of the Association of the Arab-American University Graduates. Chicago, Ill., 17–19 Oct., 1975.
86. Middle East Studies Association. Ninth Annual Meeting, Louisville, Ky., 19–22 Nov., 1975.

87. Seminar on Development of Human Resources: The Role of Women in Jordan. Jordan, 1975.

88. Seminar on the Role of Women in Integrated Rural Development with Emphasis on Population Problems. Cairo, 1974. Report of the Seminar on the Role of Women in Integrated Rural Development with Emphasis on Population Problems. Rome: FAO, 1975.

89. Seminar on the Status of Woman in the Islamic Family. International Islamic Center for Population Studies and Research, Al-Azhar University, Cairo, Egypt, 20–22 Dec., 1975.

90. Middle East Studies Association Tenth Annual Meeting: Panel on Women and Modern Secular Education in the Near East. Los Angeles, 10–13 Nov., 1976.

91. Second Symposium on Manpower Development. Proceedings of the Second Symposium on Manpower Development: The Role of the Jordanian Woman. Amman, Jordan, 4–7 Apr., 1976.

92. Wellesley Conference on Women and Development. Wellesley College, Mass., 2–6 June, 1976. Sponsored by: African Studies Association, Center for Research on Women; Association for Asian Studies; and Latin American Studies Association, Center for Research on Women. (Résumé in *Women's International Network News* 2, 3 (Summer, 1976): 11–14.)

93. Wingspread Meeting, following the Wellesley College Conference, Wisconsin, 7–10 June, 1976. (Résumé of Conference in *Women's International Network News* 2, 3 (Summer, 1976): 14–15.)

94. International Political Science Association (IPSA) Congress. Edinburgh, 16–21 Aug., 1976.

95. Association of the Arab-American University Graduates. Ninth Annual Convention on Development in the Arab World. New York, 1–3 Oct., 1976.

96. Middle East Institute Annual Conference on the Process of Development in the Middle East: Goals and Achievements. Washington, D.C., 15–16 Oct., 1976.

97. National Congress of Sudanese Women's Union. Sudan, 20–24 Apr., 1976. (Resumé in *Women's International Network News* 2, 4 (Autumn 1976): 54.)

98. Organization for the Promotion of Social Sciences in the Middle East (OPSSME). Third Workshop on Family and Kinship. Sponsored by: Kuwait University and UNESCO. Kuwait, 27–30 Nov., 1976.

99. Seminar on the Muslim Woman—Her Full Potential. Organized by the International Federation of Business and Professional Women in Collaboration with the International Planned Parenthood Federation. Rabat, Morocco, 8–11 Jan., 1977.

100. Sixth Biennial Conference on Society and the Sexes in Medieval Islam. Gustave E. Von Grunebaum Center for Near Eastern Studies, University of California, Los Angeles, 13–15 May, 1977.

101. Conference on Women in Management. Sponsored by: Graduate Management Program, American University of Cairo; School of Commerce, Cairo University; and Academy of International Business, Cairo, Egypt, 21–23 May, 1977.

102. National Women's Union of Tunisia. Family Planning and Women's Development Programs. Monastir, Tunis, 9–12 Aug., 1977.

102a. United Nations. World Health Organization. Seminar on Traditional Practices Affecting the Health of Women. Khartoum, Sudan, 4–8 Feb., 1979.

Women in Islam
and the Law

103. Abassi, A. de Zayas, 'Women in Islam.' *Islamic Literature* 5 (Feb. 1953):119–125; 6 (Jan. 1954): 55–61.
104. Abbott, Nabia. *Aisha, the Beloved of Muhammad.* Chicago: University of Chicago, 1942.
105. Abbott, Nabia. 'Women and the State in Early Islam.' *Journal of Near Eastern Studies* 1 (1942):106–126, 341–368.
106. Abdel-Ati, Hammudah. 'The Family Structure in Islam.' Ph.D. dissertation, Princeton University, 1971.
107. Abdel Hamid, Ibrahim. 'Dissolution of Marriage in Islamic Law.' *Islamic Quarterly* 3 (1956–57):166–175, 215–223; 4 (1957):3–10, 57–65, 97–113.
108. Abdel Rahman, Aisha. 'The Personality of Woman in the Quran.' Paper presented at the Seminar on the Status of Woman in the Islamic Family, International Islamic Center for Population Studies and Research, Al-Azhar University, Cairo, Egypt, 20–22 Dec., 1975.
109. Abdul, Khalik. 'Marriage in Islam.' *Pakistan Philosophical Journal* 4, 7 (1963):51–64.
111. Abdul Rauf, Mohammad. *Marriage in Islam.* New York; Exposition Press, 1972.
112. Accad, Evelyne. 'The Veil of Shame.' *Women's International Network News* 3, 3 (Summer 1977):52–54.
113. Afza, N. 'Woman in Islam.' *Islamic Literature* 13, 10

(1967):5–24. (Also in *Muslim News* 6, 8 (Feb. 1968):30–33.)

114. Afzal, M., Bean, Lee L. and Husain, I. 'Muslim Marriages: Age, Mehr and Social Status.' *Pakistan Development Review* 12 (1973):48–61.

115. 'Aisha, Mother of the Faithful.' *Arab World* 7, 6 (1961).

116. El-Akel, Abderrazak. 'Derecho conyugal o derechos de la mujer en el Islam.' (Resumen de la Tesis Doctoral.) *Cuadernos de la Biblioteca Española de Tetuan* 8 (1973):87–103.

117. Ali, M. 'Changes in Muslim Personal Law: Scope and Procedure.' *Islamic Thought* 14, 2 (1970):1–15.

118. Ali, M. 'The Prophet Muhammad's Marriages.' *Islamic Review and Arab Affairs* 58, 2 (1970):7–11.

119. Ali, Mukti. 'The Position of Woman in Islamic Family.' Paper presented at the Seminar on the Status of Woman in the Islamic Family, International Islamic Center for Population Studies and Research, Al-Azhar University, Cairo, Egypt, 20–22 Dec., 1975.

120. Ali, Parveen Shaukat. 'Muslim Women Enter a New Era.' *Asian Women's Institute Newsletter* (May 1977):1–2, 5.

121. Ali, Parveen Shaukat. *Status of Women in the Muslim World: a Study in the Feminist Movements in Turkey, Egypt, Iran and Pakistan*. Lahore: Aziz Publishers, 1975.

122. Allman, James, ed. *Women's Status and Fertility in the Muslim World*. New York, Praeger, 1978.

123. Alwaye, Mohieddin. 'The Status of Women in Islam.' *Majallat Al-Azhar* 47, 4 (1975):1–5.

124. Amiruddin, Begum Sultan Mir. 'Woman's Status in Islam. A Moslem View.' *Muslim World* 28 (1938): 153–163.

125. Anderson, J.N.D. 'The Contract of Marriage.' *Muslim World* 41 (Apr. 1951):113–126.

126. Anderson, J.N.D. 'The Dissolution of Marriage.' *Muslim World* 41 (Oct. 1951):271–288.

127. Anderson, J.N.D. 'Invalid and Void Marriages in

B

Hanafi Law.' *Bulletin of the School of Oriental and African Studies* 13 (1950):357–366.

128. Anderson, J.N.D. *Islamic Law in the Modern World.* New York: New York University Press, 1959.

129. Anderson, J.N.D. 'The Problem of Divorce in the Sharia Law of Islam.' *Royal Central Asian Journal* (Apr. 1950):169–185.

130. Anderson, J.N.D. 'Reforms in the Law of Divorce in the Muslim World.' *Studia Islamica* 31 (1970): 41–52.

131. Anderson, J.N.D. 'The Role of Personal Statutes in Social Development in Islamic Countries.' *Comparative Studies in Society and History* 13, 1 (1971): 16–31.

132. Anderson, Norman. *Law Reform in the Muslim World.* London: Athlone Press, 1976.

133. Arnaldez, Roger. 'Le Coran et l'émancipation de la femme.' Paper presented at the Semaine de la Pensée Marxiste, Lyon, 4–10 Feb. Paris: La Palatine, 1965.

134. Awad, B.A. 'The Status of Women in Islam.' *Islamic Quarterly* 8 (1964):17–24.

135. Badawi, Gamal A. 'Polygamy in Islam.' *Al-Ittihad* 9 (Jan. 1972):19–23.

136. Badawi, Gamal A. 'Status of Women in Islam.' *Al-Ittihad* 8 (Sept. 1971):7–15.

137. Badran, Aida. 'The Status of Woman in Islamic Sharia.' B.A. thesis, Faculty of Arts and Sciences, American University of Cairo, 1953.

138. Badran, Hoda. 'The Problems of Women and Recommendations of the International Women's Year Conference as Related to this Region.' Paper presented at the Seminar on the Status of Woman in the Islamic Family, International Islamic Center for Population Studies and Research, Al-Azhar University, Cairo, Egypt, 20–22 Dec., 1975.

139. Barroudy, A. *The Women of the Koran.* New York: New York University, 1909.

140. Baveja, Malik R. *Women in Islam.* Agpura: Institute of Indo-Middle East Cultural Studies, n.d.

141. Bearani, Hourieh Sha'ami. 'Druze Women on the Move: Reflections of a Pioneer.' *Kidma* 2, 3 (1975): 34–35.

142. Beck, Lois. 'Women and Islam: The Impact of Religious Ideology.' Paper presented at the Wellesley Conference on Women and Development, Wellesley College, Mass., 2–6 June, 1976.

143. Beck, Lois and Keddie, Nikki, eds. *Women in the Muslim World.* Cambridge, Mass.: Harvard University Press, 1978.

144. Ben Abdalla. 'L'Islam et la condition féminine.' *Monde non-Chrétien* 47–48 (1958): 185–203.

145. Benabed, H.H. 'La condition de la femme musulmane.' *L'Islam et l'Occident* (1947): 211–219. (Also in *Cahiers du Sud* (1947): 211–220.)

146. Berlas, N.H. 'Position of Woman in Islam.' *Islamic Review* (May 1935): 187–198.

147. Bint al Shati' (Aisha Abdel Rahman). *The Wives of the Prophet.* Lahore: Ashraf, 1971.

148. Bittari, Zoubeida. *O mes soeurs musulmanes, pleurez!* Paris: Gallimard, 1964.

149. Bonnet-Eymard, J. 'Acceuil ou refus des valeurs religieuses.' *Travaux et Jours* no. 9 (1963): 45–53.

150. Borrmans, Maurice. 'Statut personnel et droit familial en pays musulmans.' *Proche-Orient Chrétien* 23 (1973): 133–147.

151. Bouhdiba, Abdel Wahab. *A la recherche des normes perdues.* Tunis: Maison Tunisienne de l'Edition, 1973.

152. Bouhdiba, Abdel Wahab. *La sexualité en Islam.* Paris: Presses Universitaires, 1975.

153. Bouhdiba, Abdel Wahab. 'Islam et sexualité.' Thèse, Université de Paris, 1972.

154. Bousquet, George-Henri. *La morale de l'Islam et son éthique sexuelle.* Paris: Maisonneuve, 1953.

155. Bousquet, George-Henri. *L'éthique sexuelle de l'Islam.* Paris: Maisonneuve and Larose, 1966.

156. Bousquet, George-Henri. *Précis élémentaire de droit musulman.* Paris: Geuthner, 1935.

157. Bousquet, George-Henri and Jahier, H. 'Les vices

rédhibitoires de la femme en droit musulman: remarques juridicomédicales.' *Revue Algérienne* Part I (1951): 52–58.

158. Brunschvig, R. 'De la filiation maternelle en droit musulman.' *Studia Islamica* 9 (1958): 49–60.

159. Castagné, J. 'Le mouvement d'émancipation de la femme musulmane en Orient.' *Revue du Monde Musulman* 43 (1921): 261. (Also in *Revue des Etudes Islamiques* 3 (1929): 161–226.)

160. Centre d'Etudes pour le Monde Arabe Moderne Reports. *Islamic Law and Change in Arab Society.* Beirut: Dar el-Mashreq, 1976.

161. Chamberlayne, J. 'The Family in Islam.' *Numen* 15 (1968): 119–141.

162. Charnay, J. P. 'La musulmane dans la ville moderne.' *Politique Etrangère* 36, 2 (1971): 141–146.

163. Chehata, Chafik. 'Le droit de répudiation (Talaq) dans le droit positif des Pays Arabes.' *Proceedings of the 27th International Congress of Orientalists* 1967 (1971): 249–250.

164. Chehata, Chafik. 'La Famille en Islam: problèmes d'actualité.' *Revue Juridique et Politique, Indépendance et Coopération* 28 (1974): 663–72.

165. Chehata, Chafik. 'Note de droit musulman sur les mariages mixtes.' *Revue Juridique et Politique, Indépendenance et Coopération* 30 (Jan.–Mar. 1976): 130–134.

166. Chelhod, Joseph. *Introduction à la sociologie de l'Islam: de l'animisme à l'universalisme.* Paris: G.P. Maisonneuve, 1958.

167. Citrine, Malika. 'Islam and the Emancipation of Women.' *Ramadan Review*, 1966.

168. Cohen, R. 'Dominance and Defiance, a Study of Marital Instability: an Islamic Society.' *Anthropological Studies* no. 6 (1971).

169. 'Le commentaire de Razi et du Manar à propos du verset coranique (2,228) sur l'égalité des droits entre les époux et sur la préeminence de l'homme.' (Mimeographed.)

170. 'The Control of Divorce.' *World Muslim League Magazine* 3, 11 (1967): 52–62.

171. Corti, Ghannam L. 'L'emancipazione della donna nell'-Iraq.' (Emancipation of Women in Iraq.) *Oriente Moderno* 33, 6 (1953):297.
172. Coulson N.J. *Succession in the Muslim Family.* London: Cambridge University Press, 1971.
173. Crabitis, P. 'Things Muhammad did for Women.' *Asia* 27 (Jan. 1927):44.
174. 'Customs: Social Status of Women is Changing in Islam.' *Life*, 9 May, 1955, pp. 80–81.
175. 'Decisions and Recommendations of the 8th Congress of the General Federation of Arab Women, Baghdad, 10–13 May, 1975.' Translated by Dr. S. Khairallah in Centre d'Etudes pour le Monde Arabe Moderne Reports, *Islamic Law and Change in Arab Society.* Beirut: Dar el-Mashreq Publications, 1976, pp. 171–177.
176. 'Daughters of the Prophet.' *Time* 18 Aug., 1952, pp. 22.
177. Daura, Bello. 'The Limit of Polygamy in Islam.' *Journal of Islamic and Comparative Law* 3 (1969): 21–26.
178. Debèche, Djamila. 'L'émancipation de la femme musulmane.' Conférence donnée au Cercle Lélian, 1 June, 1948.
179. Debèche, Djamila. 'La femme musulmane dans la société.' Conférence donnée au Centre d'Action Intellectuelle Française, 26 Apr., 1945. *Contacts en Terres d'Afrique* (1946):141–161, 7–241.
180. Debèche, Djamila. 'La femme et la condition juridique en pays d'Islam.' *Dialogues* no. 7 (Jan. 1964):20–35.
181. Decroux, Paul. 'Féminisme en Islam: la femme dans l'Islam moderne.' *Revue Juridique et Politique, Indépendance et Coopération* 23 (1968):893–908.
182. Desportes, E. 'Le droit de Djebr.' *Revue Algérienne* (1949):109–119.
183. Desportes, E. 'Théorie de la dot en droit musulman et dans les coutumes berbères.' *Revue Algérienne* Part I (1949):13–38.
184. Devereux, Robert. 'XIth Century Muslim Views on Women, Marriage, Love and Sex.' *Central Asiatic Journal* 11 (1966):134–140.

185. 'Divorce in the Moslem World.' *Middle East* (March 1978.) (Also in *WIN News* 4, 2 (Spring 1978):64–66.)
186. Djebar, Assia. *Women of Islam.* London: André Deutsch, 1961. (Original title: *Femmes d'Islam.*)
187. Donaldson, D.M. 'Temporary Marriage in Islam.' *Muslim World* 26 (1936):358–364.
188. Ehrenfels, U.R. 'Ambivalent Attitudes to Womanhood in Islamic Society.' *Islamic Culture* 25 (Jan.–Oct. 1951):73–88.
189. Ehrenfels, U.R. 'Muslim Women in Present-Day Europe.' *Islamic Culture* 10 (1936):471–476.
190. Esposito, J. 'The Changing Role of Muslim Women.' *Islam and the Modern Age* 7, 1 (1976):29–56.
191. Esposito, J. 'Muslim Family Law Reform: Toward an Islamic Methodology.' *Islamic Studies* 15 (Spring 1976):19–51.
192. Esposito, J. 'Women's Rights in Islam.' *Islamic Studies* 14, 2 (Summer 1975):99–114.
193. Fahmy, M. *La condition de la femme dans la tradition et l'évolution de l'islamisme.* Paris: Félix Alcan, 1913.
194. Farman-Farmaian, Sattareh. 'Early Marriage and Pregnancy in Traditional Islamic Society.' In: *Draper World Population Fund Report: Mothers Too Soon* (Autumn 1975):6.
195. Farrag, O.L. 'A Moslem View of Sexuality.' Paper presented at the World Council of Churches Department on Cooperation of Men and Women in Church, Family and Society-Family Life Education Consultation, Geneva, 18–23 Oct., 1970.
196. Al-Faruqi, Lamia. 'Women's Rights and the Muslim Women.' *Islam and the Modern Age* 3, 2 (1972):76–99.
197. Fattal, Antoine. 'Evolution et tradition dans l'Islam actuel: à propos des droits de la femme.' Caire, Egypte, *Articles et documents de la Bibliothèque de la Documentation Française,* 15 July, 1952.
198. 'Féminisme et institutions musulmanes.' *Rayon d'Egypte* no. 28, 10 July, 1938.
199. 'La femme musulmane.' *Cahiers Nord-Africains* no. 27 (1952).

200. 'La femme musulmane. La femme dans le mariage musulman selon le rite malekite. Les données actuelles (Kabylie). Signes et causes d'évolution par manière de témoignage.' *Etudes Sociales Nord-Africaines* 27 (Dec. 1952): 58.

201. Flory, Vera E. 'Women and Culture in Islam.' *Muslim World* 30 (1940): 14–19.

202. Foca, R. 'Modernisme en Islam.' *En Terre d'Islam* no. 43 (1931): 2–11.

203. El-Garh, M. 'The Islamic Attitude Towards Women.' *Orita* no. 10 (1976): 24–45.

204. Gaudio, Attilio. *La révolution des femmes en Islam.* Paris: Julliard, 1957.

205. Gauthier, E.F. *Moeurs et coutumes des musulmans.* Paris: Payot, 1931.

206. Geertz, Clifford. *Islam Observed.* New Haven, Conn.: Yale University Press, 1968.

207. Geniaux, C. 'L'évolution des femmes musulmanes.' *Revue Politique et Parlementaire* 10, 4 (1920): 195–200.

208. Gibb, Sir Hamilton. 'The Muslim Woman in Transition.' *Sociologus* 7, 1 (1957): 92–93.

209. Gibb, Sir Hamilton. 'Women and the Law. Colloque sur la sociologie musulmane.' *Correspondance d'Orient, Actes* (Brussels) (11–14 Sept., 1961): 233–248.

210. Le Grand Mufti d'Egypte. 'L'Islam et les droits de la femme.' *Articles et Documents de la Bibliothèque de la Documentation Française,* le Caire, Egypte, May 1952.

211. Graziani, J. 'The Status of Women in the Contemporary Muslim Arab Family.' *Middle East Review* 9, 2 (Winter 1976–77).

212. Al-Haddad, Tahir. 'Notre femme dans la loi et dans la société.' Translated and analysed by M. Mutafarrij. *Revue des Etudes Islamiques* 9 (1935): 201–230.

213. Haddad, William and Aboutalib, Sofy. 'Le statut légal de la femme musulmane dans plusieurs pays du Moyen-Orient.' Beirut: United Nations, Economic and Social Office, 1972.

214. Haddad, Yvonne. 'The image of Women in Contemporary Muslim Literature.' Paper presented at a Workshop on the Status and Role of Women in Contemporary Muslim Societies, Center for the Study of World Religions, Harvard University, Cambridge, Mass., 19 April, 1975.

215. Hamid, H.A. 'Islam and the Progress of Pornography in Modern Society.' *Islamic Review* (Oct., Nov., Dec. 1962):5–7.

216. Hartmann, M. 'Woman in Islam.' *Muslim World* 4 (1914):258–265.

217. Hasan, Masud. *Daughters of Islam: Being Short Biographical Sketches of 82 Famous Muslim Women.* Lahore: Hazat Data Baksh Academy, 1976.

218. Hashim, A. 'Muslim View of the Family and the Place of Women in Islamic Society.' *Islamic Review* (Apr. 1962):20–22.

219. Hayes, H.E.E. 'Woman's Place in Islam and British Law.' *Muslim World* 7 (1917):127–130.

220. Hinchcliffe, D. 'Polygamy in Traditional and Contemporary Islamic Law.' *Islam and the Modern Age* 1 (1970):13–38.

221. Hobbalah, Mahmoud. 'Marriage, Divorce and Inheritance in Islamic Law.' *George Washington Law Review* 22 (Oct. 1953):24–31.

222. Howard, I. ' "Muta" Marriage Reconsidered in the Context of the Formal Procedures for Islamic Marriage.' *Journal of Semitic Studies* 20, 1 (1975): 82–92.

223. Hussain, Mohammad A. ' "Marriage and Khula" in Islam.' *Islam and the Modern Age* 9, 2 (May 1978):86–88.

224. Hussein, Aziza. 'Status of Women in Family Law in the United Arab Republic.' Paper presented at the United Nations Seminar on Women in the Family, Lomé, Togo, 1964.

225. Hussein, Aziza. *Women in the Moslem World.* Washington, D.C.: Egyptian Embassy, 1956. (Based on a lecture delivered by Aziza Hussein at the University of Chicago, June 1954.)

226. Ibn ou Alfourat. 'Quelques réflexions sur la femme musulmane à travers les âges.' *L'Afrique et l'Asie* no. 3 (1960):46–50.

227. Idris, H.R. 'Le mariage en Occident musulman.' *Studia Islamica* 32 (1970):157–167.

228. Idris, H.R. 'Le mariage en Occident musulman—analyse de fatwas médiévales extraites du "Mi'yar" d'Al-Wancharichi.' *Revue de l'Occident Musulman et de la Méditerranée* no. 12 (2ème sem. 1972): 45–62.

229. INTERCOM. Center for Global Perspectives. *Secluded at Home: Muslim Women.* Washington, D.C.: INTERCOM, 1976.

230. Jameelah, Maryam. *Islam and the Muslim Woman Today: The Muslim Woman and her Role in Society, Duties of the Muslim Mother*...Lahore: Mohammad Yusuf Khan, 1976.

231. Jennings, R.C. 'Woman in Early 17th Century Ottoman Judicial Records—the Sharia Court of Anatolian Kayseri.' *Journal of the Economic and Social History of the Orient* (JESHO) 18 (1975):53–114.

232. Kamel, Abdel Aziz. 'The Role of Woman in the Building of the First Islamic Society.' Paper presented at the Seminar on the Status of Woman in the Islamic Family, International Islamic Center for Population Studies and Research, Al-Azhar University, Cairo, Egypt, 20–22 Dec., 1975.

233. Karmi, H.S. 'The Family as a Developing Social Group in Islam.' *Asian Affairs* 6 (1975):61–68.

234. Karoui Chabbi, Belgacem. 'Réflexions sur la condition juridique de la femme arabo-musulmane: matriarcat et concubinage.' *Revue Juridique et Politique, Indépendance et Coopération* 28, 4 (Oct.–Dec. 1974): 558–569.

235. Keddie, Nikki R. *Scholars, Saints and Sufis: Muslim Religious Institutions Since 1500.* Berkeley: University of California Press, 1972.

236. Khalafallah, Mohammad A. 'Woman in Contemporary Islamic Society.' Translated by S. Khairallah in Centre d'Etudes pour le Monde Arabe Moderne

Reports, *Islamic Law and Change in Arab Society*.
Beirut: Dar al Machreq Publications, 1976, pp.
179–186.

237. Khayat, Abdel Aziz.' An Islamic Viewpoint on the
Concept of Association of Both Sexes and its
Rules.' Paper presented at the Seminar on the Status
of Women in the Islamic Family, International
Center for Population Studies and Research,
Al-Azhar University, Cairo, Egypt, 20–22 Dec.,
1975.

238. Korson, J.H. 'Dowry and Social Class in an Urban
Muslim Community.' *Journal of Marriage and the
Family* 29 (Spring 1967):527–533.

239. Lammens, H. 'Un document sur les revendications
féministes en terre d'Islam.' *En Terre d'Islam*
(1933):233–238.

240. Lapanne-Joinville, J. 'A propos de l'ifâf.' *Revue
Algérienne* Part I (1949):119–120.

241. Lapanne-Joinville, J. 'Le régime des biens entre époux
(dans le rite malékite).' *Revue Marocaine de Droit*
(1950):394–406.

242. Lapanne-Joinville, J. 'La rescision du mariage en droit
musulman malékite.' *Revue Marocaine de Droit*
(1952):431–450.

243. Lapanne-Joinville, J. 'La théorie des nullités de mariage
en droit musulman malékite.' *Revue Algérienne*
Part I (1951):92–102.

244. Larguesche, H. 'Un manifeste féministe musulman.' *En
Terre d'Islam* (1928):172–185.

245. Layish, Aharon. 'Woman and Succession in the Muslim
Family in Israel.' *Asian and African Studies* (Jerusalem) 9 (1973):23–62.

246. Layish, Aharon. *Women and Islamic Law in a non-
Muslim State*. New York: Halsted Press, 1975.

247. Lemu, Aisha and Heeren, F. 'Women in Islam.' Paper
delivered at the International Islamic Conference
of the Islamic Council of Europe, London, 3–12
Apr., 1976. (Published London, Islamic Foundation,
1976.)

248. Levy, Reuben. *Social Structure of Islam*, 2nd edn of *The*

Sociology of Islam. Cambridge: Cambridge University Press, 1967.

249. Lodi, Z. 'Study of the Status of the Married Woman in the Roman Law, English Common Law, Church Law and Islamic Law.' *Islamic Review and Arab Affairs* 53, 10–11 (1970):26–29.

250. Lorear, A. 'La condition de la femme en Islam et son évolution.' *Le Droit des Femmes* (May 1954):14.

251. Lucman, T.A. 'The Role of Muslim Woman in Public Life.' Paper presented at the Seminar on the Status of Woman in the Islamic Family, International Islamic Center for Population Studies and Research, Al-Azhar University, Cairo, Egypt, 20–22 Dec., 1975.

252. Malhas, Thurayya. 'The Moslem Arab Woman and her Rights.' Paper translated by Nuha Salibi, 1971.

253. Malik, Fida Hussein. *Wives of the Prophet.* Lahore: Kashmiri Bazar, 1961.

254. Malika, Cirrine. 'Islam and the Emancipation of Women.' *Islamic Review* (Nov.–Dec. 1965):34–69.

255. 'Un manifeste féministe musulman.' *En Terre d'Islam* (1928):172–185.

256. Maudidi, S. Abdul A'la. *Purdah and the Status of Women in Islam.* Lahore, 1972.

257. Mohamed, Ahmed Zaki. 'Certains aspects des relations conjugales. Leurs particularités en droit musulman.' *L'Egypte Contemporaine* 58 (1967):79–124.

258. Mohanna, Ahmed I. 'Woman's Position in Islam.' *Majallat Al-Azhar* (Oct. 1968):11–13; (Dec. 1968): 9–12; (Jan. 1969):5–7; (Feb. 1969):5–8, 9–12; (Apr. 1969):6–9; (May 1969):9–12.

259. Monteil, Vincent. *Le monde musulman.* Paris: Horizons de France, 1963.

260. Monteil, Vincent. 'Le progrès des femmes en Afrique noire musulmane.' *L'Islam Noire* (1964):149–183.

261. 'Muslim Women Declare Change in Muslim Personal Law Will not be Tolerated.' (Conference Held in Bombay.) *Muslim Digest* 24, 1 (1973):5–9.

262. 'The Muslim Women of Syria and Pakistan.' *Islamic Review* 39 (Oct. 1951):38–39.

263. Nallino, C.A. 'Il velo delle donne e i Wahhabiti.' (The

Quranic Origins of the Principle of the Veil for Women in the Wahhabite Doctrine.) *Oriente Moderno* 6, 6 (1926): 338–339.

264. National Council of Lebanese Women. 'The Status of Women in Arab Laws in the Light of U.N. International Conventions.' Studies and Recommendations Issued at the Seminar Held by the National Council of Lebanese Women, Beirut, 22–31 May, 1974.

265. Nazat, Afra. 'Women in Islam.' *Islamic Literature* 13 (1967): 5–24.

266. Neal, Shirley W.Z. 'Family Relationship in the Revolt of Islam.' Ph.D. dissertation, University of Illinois, 1973.

267. Nejjari, F. 'Dans quelle mesure existe-t-il une égalité entre hommes et femmes en Islam?' *La Pensée* 1, 1 (1962): 35–40.

268. Niazi, Kausar. *Creation of Man.* Lahore: Shaikh Mohammad Ashraf, Kashmiri Bazar, 1975.

269. Niazi, Kausar. 'Marriage with the People of the Book.' *Islamic Literature* 17, 7 (1971): 13–21.

270. Niazi, Kausar. *Modern Challenges Faced by Muslim Families.* Islamabad: Islamic Research Institute Press, 1975.

271. Niazi, Kausar. *Modern Challenges to Muslim Families.* Lahore: Shaikh Mohammad Ashraf, Kashmiri Bazar, 1976.

272. Norès, E. 'Etude sur le don moutaa ou don de consolation.' *Revue Algérienne* Part I (1928): 1–13.

273. Nyland, P. 'Women in Judaism and Islam.' *Muslim World* 6 (1916): 291–295.

274. Papanek, Hanna. 'Purdah: Separate Worlds and Symbolic Shelter.' *Comparative Studies in Society and History* 15, 3 (1973): 289–325.

275. Pastner, Carroll. 'Accommodations to Purdah: The Female Perspective.' *Journal of Marriage and the Family* 36, 2 (1974): 408–414.

276. Pastner, Carroll. 'A Social Structural and Historical Analysis of Honor, Shame and Purdah.' *Anthropological Quarterly* 45, 4 (1972): 248–261.

277. Peale, Octave. *La femme musulmane dans le droit, la religion et les moeurs.* Rabat: Les Editions la Porte, 1946.

278. Pittman, C.R. 'In Defense of the Veil.' *Muslim World* 33 (1943):203–212.

279. Qadri, M.S.A. 'Polygamy.' *Islamic Thought* 14, 1 (1970):1–17.

280. Rafiq, B.A. *The Status of Woman in Islam.* London: Orchard, n.d.

281. Rafiullah, Abu Shihab. 'A note on Political Influence on the Practice of Divorce.' *Islamic Studies* 5 (1966): 99–104.

282. Ramadan, Said. 'The Plight of Womenfolk in Muslim Society.' *Muslim Digest* (Nov. 1962):7–13.

283. Rashed, Zeinab. 'Social Responsibility of Woman in Islam.' Paper presented at the Seminar on the Status of Woman in the Islamic Family, International Islamic Center for Population Studies and Research, Al-Azhar University, Cairo, Egypt, 20–22 Dec., 1975.

284. Rauf, M.A. *The Islamic View of Women and the Family.* New York: Robert Speller and Sons, 1977.

285. Rejwan, Nissim. 'Women and Islamic Law in a Non-Muslim State.' *Jerusalem Post Magazine,* 8 Apr. (1977):13.

286. Raza, S.M. 'Changing Purdah System in Muslim Society.' *Islam in the Modern Age,* 74 (1975):40–56.

287. Reza-ur-Rahim. 'A Reconstruction of the Procedure of Divorce according to the Holy Quran.' *Islam and the Modern Age* 7, 2 (1976):5–14.

288. Roberts, Robert. *The Social Laws of the Quran: Considered and Compared with those of the Hebrew and other Ancient Codes.* New Delhi: Kitab Bhavan, 1977.

289. Rosen, Lawrence. 'I Divorce Thee.' *Transaction* 7, 8 (1970):34–37.

290. Rosenthal, Franz. 'Fiction and Reality: Sources for Role of Sex in Islam.' Paper presented at the Sixth Biennial Conference on Society and the Sexes in Medieval Islam, Gustave E. Von Grunebaum

Center for Near Eastern Studies, University of California, Los Angeles, 13–15 May, 1977.

291. Rossi, E. 'Polemica in Egitto per una proposta di equiparare le donne agli uomini nelle successioni di diritto musulmano.' (Polemics in Egypt Against a Project for the Equality of Men and Women in Matters of Succession in Muslim Law.) *Oriente Moderno* 9, 1 (1929): 53–54.

292. Rouhani, Dr. 'Personnalité de la femme en Islam.' *Pensée Chiite* no. 1 (1960): 27–36; no. 2 (1960): 21–30; no. 3 (1960): 31–36.

293. 'Round Table on Women in Islamic Society.' (In Japanese.) *Chûtô-tsûhô* 246 (Feb. 1977): 2–16.

294. Rynty, Carol J. 'The Role of Women in the Muslim Middle East.' Ph.D. dissertation, University of Nebraska, 1976.

295. Safwad, Osman. 'Contradiction entre situation de fait et situation de droit concérnant la femme dans les pays arabes.' *Revue Algérienne des Sciences Juridiques, Economiques et Politiques* 11 (1974): 113–117.

296. Saleh, Saneya A.W. 'Women in Islam: Comments and Clarifications.' Paper presented at the Center of Continuing Education of Women, University of California, Berkeley, 8, 11, 13, 14 and 15 Oct., n.d.

297. Saleh, Saneya A.W. 'Women in Islam: their status in Religious and Traditional Culture.' *International Journal of Sociology of the Family* 2, 1 (Mar. 1972): 35–42.

298. Saleh, Saneya A.W. 'Women in Islam: their Role in Religious and Traditional Culture.' *International Journal of Sociology of the Family* 2, 2 (Sept. 1972): 193–201.

299. Saleh, Sheikh Subhi. 'The Status of the Moslem Woman between Traditions and Islamic Personal Statutes.' Lecture presented in the course Women in the Arab World offered by the Institute for Women's Studies in the Arab World at the Beirut University College, 1979. (Mimeographed.)

300. Salman, A.M.M. 'Polygamy and the Status of Women in Islamic Society.' *Majallat al-Azhar* 33, 1 (1961): 17–24.

301. Sammari, Mohammad S.R. 'Réflexion sur la condition de la femme en droit musulman.' *Revue Juridique et Politique, Indépendance et Coopération* 28 (1974): 548–557.

302. El-Sayed, D.H. 'The Institution of Marriage in Islam.' *Journal of Islamic Studies* 1 (1968): 45–87.

303. Schacht, J. 'Adultery as an Impediment to Marriage in Islamic and in Canon Law.' *Archives d'Histoire du Droit Oriental* 1 (2ème sem. 1952): 105–123.

304. Shaltout, Mahmoud. 'The Position of Women in Islam.' *Majallat al-Azhar* 32, 7 (1960): 6–23.

305. Shaltout, Mahmoud. *The Quran and Woman.* Cairo: International Islamic Center for Population Studies and Research, Al-Azhar University, 1975.

306. Shanan, Naadirah. 'The Muslim Woman and the Imamate.' *Islamic Review and Arab Affairs* (Formerly *Islamic Review*) 53, 5 (1965): 24–28.

307. Shepherd, E.R. 'Moslem Wife.' *Cosmopolitan*, Nov. 1956. pp. 60–63.

308. Siddiqui, M.M. *Women in Islam.* Lahore: Institute of Islamic Culture, 1966; New York: Orientalia, 1969.

309. Smith, J. and Haddad, Y. 'Women in the Afterlife: The Islamic View as Seen from Quran and Tradition.' *Journal of the American Academy of Religion* 43, 1 (1975): 39–50.

310. Smith, Margaret. *Rābi'a the Mystic and her Fellow Saints in Islam: Being The Life and Teachings of Rābi'a al-'Adawiyya al-Qaysiyya of Basra, together with some Account of the Place of Women Saints in Islam.* Cambridge: Cambridge University Press, 1928.

311. Soorma, C.A. 'Islam's Attitude towards Women and Orphans.' *Islamic Review* 17, 1 (1929): 72–75.

312. Stern, Gertrude H. *Marriage in Early Islam.* James G. Forlong Fund, Vol. 18. London: Royal Asiatic Society, 1939.

313. Sukhdev Singh. 'Development of the Concept of Divorce in Muslim Law.' *Allahabad Law Review* 5 (1973):117–127.
314. Swan, G. 'Monogamy in Islam.' *Muslim World* 3 (1913):75–77.
315. Taalbi, M. 'L'Islam classique et la femme.' Communication inédite au 3ème Seminaire de Sociologie sur les Mutations Actuelles de la Famille au Maghreb, Tunis, Dec. 1966.
316. Tabbara, Sajida. 'A Comparative, Documentary and Analytical Study of the Position and Rights of Women in Islam.' Beirut University College, Beirut, Lebanon, 1974.
317. United Nations. Economic Commission for Western Asia. 'Projet d'étude—Le statut légal de la femme musulmane dans les pays de la région de l'ECWA' (E/ECWA/POP/WP.2), Mar. 1976.
318. United Nations. UNESOB (Bureau des Affaires de de l'ONU à Beyrouth). 'Le statut légal de la femme musulmane dans plusieurs pays du moyen orient' (ESOB/DM/72/42). Beirut: UNESOB (now ECWA), Dec. 1972.
319. Vacca, V. 'Fetwa di Al-Azhar sulla participazione delle donne alla vita pubblica.' (A 'Fetwa' of Al-Azhar on the Participation of Women in Public Life.) *Oriente Moderno* 33, 1 (1953):40–41.
320. Vacca, V. 'Libro di una musulmana drusa contro il velo delle donne.' (Nazira Zein ed-Din, a Druze woman, Writes against the Use of the Veil for Women and Claims the Right to Education and Freedom.) *Oriente Moderno* 8, 10 (1928):497.
321. Van Ess, Dorothy. *Fatima and her Sisters*. New York: John Day, 1961.
322. Van Sommer, A. and Zwemer, S. *Daylight in the Harem: a New Era for Moslem Women*. Edinburgh, 1911.
323. Van Sommer, A. and Zwemer, S. *Our Moslem Sisters*. New York: Fleming-Revell, 1907.
324. Veccia-Vaglieri, L. 'Fetwà del rettorato di el-Azhar sull'obligo del velo femminile e della circoncisione a proposito delle conversioni degli "intoccabili"

indiani.' (On the Conversion of the Indian 'Untouchables': a Fatwa of Al-Azhar on the Obligation of the Veil for Women and Circumcision for Men.) *Oriente Moderno* 16, 9 (1936): 501–502.

325. Vexivière, J. and Gillet, M. 'Un manifeste féministe musulman.' *En Terre d'Islam* (1928): 172–189.

326. White, Elizabeth H. 'Purdah.' *Frontiers* 1 (Sept. 1977): 31–42.

327. Woodsmall, Ruth F. *Moslem Women Enter a New World*. London: Allen, 1936; New York: Round Table Press, 1936. (Reprinted in New York: AMS Press, 1975.)

328. Yafi, Abd. 'Condition privée de la femme dans le droit de l'Islam.' Thèse de doctorat, Paris, 1926.

329. Youssef, N. 'Education and Female Modernism in the Muslim World.' *Journal of International Affairs* 30, 2 (1976–77): 191–210.

330. Youssef, N. 'Fertility and Labor Force Patterns Among Women in Islamic Societies.' Paper presented at the Symposium of Near Eastern Women through the Ages, Berkeley, Calif., 1975.

331. Youssef, N. 'The Muslim Woman in the Midst of Political Modernization.' Sept. 1975.

332. Youssef, N. 'Women and Agricultural Production in Muslim Societies.' Paper presented at the Seminar on Prospects for Growth in Rural Societies: with or without Active Participation of Women, Agricultural Development Council, New Jersey, 1974.

333. Zikria, Nizar. 'The Status of Women in Islam.' *Journal of the Islamic Medical Association* 7, 1 (Feb. 1976): 19–21.

334. Zwemer, Samuel. *Moslem Women*. West Medford, Mass.: Central Committee on the United Study of Foreign Missions, 1926.

Women in the Arab Middle East— General Works

335. Abdallah, Ismail Sabri. 'Women and Development.' Paper presented at the Seminar on Arab Woman in National Development, sponsored by UNICEF, Arab League and Arab States Adult Functional Literacy Center, Cairo, Egypt, 24–30 Sept., 1972.

336. Abdel Fatah, Hoda. 'Women's Participation in Voluntary Organization.' Thesis, Higher Institute of Social Work, Cairo, Egypt, 1972.

337. Abdel Hamid, Naguiba. 'Factors Affecting the Role of Women in National Development.' Paper presented at the Seminar on Arab Women in National Development, sponsored by UNICEF, Arab League and Arab States Adult Functional Literacy Center, Cairo, Egypt, 24–30 Sept., 1972.

338. Abu Jaber, Faiz. 'The Status of Women in Early Arab History.' *Islam and the Modern Age* 4, 2 (1973): 67–76.

339. Abu Zahra, Nadia. 'Material Power, Honour, Friendship and the Etiquette of Visiting.' *Anthropological Quarterly* 47 (Jan. 1974): 120–38.

340. Abu Zahra, Nadia. 'On the Modesty of Women in Arab Muslim Villages: a Reply.' *American Anthropologist* 72, 5 (1970): 1079–88.

341. Accad, Evelyne. 'The Inadequate Portrayal of the Social Problems of Women in Maghreb and Mashreq Novelists.' Paper presented at the Anthropology and Literature Conference, Urbana, Ill., 1974.

342. Accad, Evelyne. 'Interrelationship between Arab Nationalism and Feminist Consciousness in the North African Novels written by Women.' *Ba-Shiru* 8, 2 (1977). (Publication of the University of Wisconsin–Madison.)

343. Accad, Evelyne. 'New Feminist Consciousness among Arab Women Novelists.' Paper presented at the Regional Women's Conference, Bloomington, Ind., 1975.

344. Accad, Evelyne. 'Role of Women in Arabic Literature.' Paper presented at the 8th Annual Convention of the Arab-American University Graduates, Chicago, Ill., 17–19 Oct., 1975.

345. Accad, Evelyne. 'Veil of Shame: Role of Women in the Modern Fiction of North Africa and the Arab World.' Ph.D. dissertation, Indiana University, 1973. In Print by Sherbrooke, Edition Naaman, Jan. 1978.

346. 'Access of Girls to School Education in the Arab States.' *Education Panorama* no. 9 (1966):23–25.

347. Adibe, N. 'Awareness of the Changing Roles of Females and Males With Implications for Classroom Instruction.' Paper presented at the 9th Annual Convention of the Association of the Arab-American University Graduates, New York, 1–3 Oct., 1976.

348. Ahdab-Yehya, May. 'Reflections on the Conference on Women and Development V.' *Signs: Journal of Women in Culture and Society* 3, 1 (Autumn 1977): 326–329.

349. Ahmed, Wajih. 'Constraints and Requirements to Increase Women's Participation in Integrated Rural Development.' Paper presented at the Seminar on the Role of Women in Integrated Rural Development with Emphasis on Population Problems, Cairo, Egypt, 26 Oct.–3 Nov., 1974.

350. Al-Amir, Daisy. 'Women's Concerns as Reflected in Contemporary Feminine Fiction Works.' Lecture presented in the course Women in the Arab World, offered by the Institute for Women's Studies in the

Arab World at the Beirut University College, 1979. (Mimeographed.)

351. Anderson, J.N.D. *Family Law in Asia and Africa.* London: Allen and Unwin, 1968.

352. Ansari, Ghaus. 'Status of Women in Different Societies: a Comparative Survey.' *Review of Ethnology* 3, 18 (1972):137–142.

353. Antoun, Richard T. 'Antoun's Reply to Abu Zahra.' *American Anthropologist* 72 (1970):1088–1092.

354. Antoun, Richard T. 'On the Modesty of Women in Arab Muslim Villages: a Study in the Accommodation of Traditions.' *American Anthropologist* 70, 4 (1968):671–697.

355. 'Appearance and Reality: Status and Roles of Women in Mediterranean Societies.' *Anthropological Quarterly* 40 (July 1967). (Special issue.)

356. Arab League. Arab States Adult Functional Literacy Center. 'Role of Arab Women in National Development. Report of a Conference.' Cairo, Egypt, 24–30 Sept., 1972.

357. Arab League. Social Department. Committee for the Status of Arab Women within the Framework of the League of Arab States. Workshops Held in 1972 and 1973, and Papers resulting from them on the Arab Woman, her Legal, Social and Economic Status.

358. Arab League. Social Department. Committee for the Status of Arab Women within the Framework of the League of Arab States. 'Report on Work and Recommendations of: First, Second and Third Sessions.' Cairo, Egypt, 22–24 Jan., 1972; 24–28 Feb., 1973 and 20–25 Jan., 1974.

359. Arab League. Social Department. Committee for the Status of Arab Women within the Framework of the League of Arab States. 'Report on the Third Meeting.' Kuwait, 4–7 Nov., 1974.

360. 'The Arab Woman, an Untypical View.' *Aramco World Magazine* (Mar./Apr., 1971):1–40.

361. 'The Arab Woman as Resource.' *Sketch* (4 Oct., 1974): 24–25.

362. 'Arabian Women's Issue.' *Aftonposten*, 3 Nov., 1972. (Swedish newspaper.)

363. Armand, M.L. 'Féminisme.' *En Terre d'Islam* no. 17 (1936):324–332.

364. Aswad, Barbara C. 'Key and Peripheral Roles of Noble Women in a Middle Eastern Plains Village.' *Anthropological Quarterly* 40, 3 (1967):139–153.

365. Ayoub, Millicent Robinson. 'Endogamous Marriage in a Middle Eastern Village.' Ph.D. dissertation, Radcliffe/Harvard University, 1957.

366. Ayoub, Millicent Robinson. 'Parallel Cousin Marriage and Endogamy: a Study in Sociometry.' *Southwestern Journal of Anthropology* 15 (1959):266–275.

367. Azzam, Henry. 'Women, Employment and Development in the Arab World.' Lecture presented in the course Women in the Arab World, offered by the Institute for Women's Studies in the Arab World at the Beirut University College, 1979. (Mimeographed.)

368. Babaa, Khalid I. 'Status of Women in the Arab World.' *Arab Studies* no. 28 (July 1972). (League of Arab States.)

369. Badran, Hoda. 'Arab Women in National Development, a Study of Three Arab Countries: Egypt, Lebanon, Sudan.' Paper presented at the Seminar on Arab Women in National Development, sponsored by UNICEF, Arab League and Arab States Adult Functional Literacy Center, Cairo, Egypt, 24–30 Sept., 1972.

370. Badran, Hoda. 'The Cost of Child.' *Ceres* (FAO) 7, 4 (1974):25–30.

371. Badran, Hoda. 'Deliberations of the International Women's Year Conference and its Relationship to the Arab Region.' Paper presented at the Seminar on the Status of Women in the Moslem Family, sponsored by the International Islamic Center for Population Studies and Research, Al-Azhar University, Cairo, Egypt, 20–22 Dec., 1975.

372. Badran, Hoda. 'A Proposed Plan of Action for the Integration of Women in Development for the

Eastern Mediterranean Region.' Paper presented at the UN World Conference for the International Women's Year, Mexico City, 19 June–2 July, 1975.

373. Badran, Hoda. 'Women Population and Integrated Rural Development.' Paper presented at the Seminar on the Role of Women in Integrated Rural Development, with Emphasis on Population Problems, Cairo, Egypt, 26 Nov.–3 Dec., 1974.

374. Baldwin, Stephen C. 'For Better, For Worse.' *People* 2, 2 (1975):25–26.

375. Barbot, M. 'Destins de femmes arabes.' *Orient* no. 31 (1964):109–128.

376. Bashshur, Munir. 'Arab Women and Education.' Lecture presented in the course Women in the Arab World, offered by the Institute for Women's Studies in the Arab World at the Beirut University College, 1979. (Mimeographed.)

377. Bateson, Mary C. and Thompson, Carolyn A. 'Women's Part in Interpersonal Quarreling and Third Person Mediation.' Paper presented at the 8th Annual Meeting of the Middle East Studies Association, Boston, 6–9 Nov., 1974.

378. Beck, Lois Grant and Keddie, N. eds. *Beyond the Veil: Women in the Middle East*. Cambridge, Mass.: Harvard University Press, 1976.

379. Beck, Dorothy Fahs. 'The Changing Moslem Family of the Middle East.' *Marriage and Family Living* 19 (Winter, 1957):340–347.

380. Berger, Morroe. 'The Arab danse du ventre.' *Dance Perspectives* 10 (1961):6–49.

381. Bickers, William M. *Harem Surgeon*. Beirut: American University of Beirut, 1976.

382. Blanch, Lesley. 'O, Speak to Me of Love! An English Woman Visits a Harem.' *Reporter* 8 (12 May, 1953):22–24.

383. Blanch, Lesley. *The Wilder Shores of Love*. New York: Simon and Schuster, 1954; London: Murray, 1954.

384. Boserup, Ester. 'The Changing Roles of Women in the Process of Development.' Paper, n.d.

385. Boserup, Ester. *Women and their Role in Peasant Societies.* London: University of London, Centre of International and Area Studies, 1974.
386. Boserup, Ester. *Women's Role in Economic Development.* London: George Allen and Unwin, 1970.
387. Boserup, Ester and Liljencrantz, Christina. *Integration of Women in Development.* United Nations Development Program, 1975.
388. Boss, Mary G. 'A New Factor in the Equation: Women and Development.' Paper presented at the Annual Conference of the Middle East Institute in conjunction with the School of Advanced International Studies of the Johns Hopkins University, on the Process of Development in the Middle East: Goals and Achievements. Summary Report. Washington, D.C., 15–16 Oct., 1976.
389. Bouhdiba, A. 'La délinquence féminine est une conséquence de l'évolution.' *L'Action,* 31 Dec., 1964.
390. Boullata, Kamal, ed. *Women of the Fertile Crescent: Modern Poetry by Arab Women.* Washington, D.C.: Three Continents Press, 1978.
391. Budiner, Melitta. *Le droit de la femme à l'égalité de salaire et la convention no. 100 de l'Organisation Internationale du Travail.* Paris: Librairie Generale de Droit et de Jurisprudence, 1975.
392. Burhil, Zoubaida. 'L'impact du travail féminin sur les relations du couple.' Doctorat du 3ème Cycle, Rabat, 1975.
393. Boutarfa, Salah el-Dine. 'Le voile.' *Revue de l'Institut des Belles Lettres Arabes* 26, 104 (4ème trim., 1963):297–321.
394. Bujra, Abdallah. 'The Relationship between the Sexes amongst the Bedouin in a Town.' Paper presented at the Mediterranean Social Science Council Conference, Athens, Greece, 1966.
395. Castillo, Gelia T. *The Changing Role of Women in Rural Societies: a Summary of Trends and Issues.* Report no. 12. New York: Agricultural Development Council, Feb. 1977.
396. Catrice, Paul. 'Femmes écrivains d'Afrique du Nord et

du Proche-Orient.' *L'Afrique et l'Asie* 59, 3 (1962): 21–44.

397. Chabaud, Jacqueline. *The Education and Advancement of Women.* Paris: UNESCO, 1970.

398. Chapoutot-Remadi, M. 'L'image de la femme dans Kalila wa Dimnah.' *Cahiers de Tunisie* 26, 91–92 (1975):17–40.

399. Charnay, J.P. 'Condition féminine et rapports sociaux.' *Cahiers de l'Orient Contemporain* 26, 78 (Dec. 1969): 4–7.

400. Charnay, J.P. 'La musulmane dans la ville moderne.' *Politique Etrangère* 36, 2 (1971):141–6.

401. Charnay, J.P. 'Stratification économique et dimensions culturelles dans les pays arabes.' Paper presented at the 9th World Congress of the International Political Science Association, Montreal, 1973.

402. Chebat, Fouad. 'La femme du diplomate arabe.' *Annales de la Faculté de Droit de Beyrouth* 55 (1968):55–58.

403. Chelhod, J. 'Le mariage avec la cousine parallèle dans le systeme arabe.' *L'Homme* 5 (July/Dec. 1965).

404. Chemali, Mona and Fadlallah, I. 'Témoignage d' étudiantes et étudiants.' *Conférence de Cénacle* 17, 5–6 (1963):53–64.

405. Clignet, R. *Many Wives, many Powers: Authority and Power in Polygamous Families.* Chicago, Ill.: Northwestern University Press, 1970.

406. 'La condition de la femme dans le Moyen-Orient arabe.' *Documentation Française* no. 2086 (10 Oct., 1955). (Notes et Etudes Documentaires.)

407. 'Conference of Arab Women, Kuwait.' *Arab Report and Record* 11 (1972):31.

408. 'Congrés féministe arabe de Beyrouth.' *Revue de Presse* Part 71 (Jan. 1963).

409. Cooper, Elizabeth. *Harim and the Purdah: Studies of Oriental Women.* Detroit: Gale, 1974. (Reprint of 1915 edition.)

410. Crapanzano, V. and Kramer, J.' A World of Saints and She-Demons; the Story of how Latifa Was Cured of her Paralysis Sheds Light on Life in a Small

Arab Town.' *New York Times Magazine* June 1969, pp. 14–38.

411. Cuisenier, Jean. 'Endogamie et exogamie dans le mariage arabe.' *L'Homme* 2, 2 (May/Aug. 1962): 80–105.

412. El-Daghestani, Kazem. 'The Evolution of the Moslem Family in the Middle Eastern Countries.' *International Social Science Bulletin* 5, 4 (1953): 681–691.

413. Danforth, Sandra C. 'Women's Political Participation in the Ottoman Empire and the Turkish Republic: a Comparative Analysis.' Paper presented at the 9th Annual Middle East Studies Association Meeting, Louisville, Ky., 19–22 Nov. 1975.

414. Darwish, Yehia H. 'Constraints and Requirements to Increase Women's Participation in Integrated Rural Development.' Paper presented at the Seminar on the Role of Women in Integrated Rural Development with Emphasis on Population Problems, Cairo, Egypt, 26 Oct.–3 Nov., 1974.

415. Daumas, Général. 'La femme arabe.' *Revue Africaine* 56 (1912): 1–154.

416. Davis, Susan S. 'Analytical Problems in the Anthropological Study of Women.' Paper presented at the 9th Annual Middle East Studies Association Meeting, Louisville, Ky., 19–22 Nov., 1975.

417. Decroux, P. 'Le droit international privé et les mariages mixtes.' *Revue Juridique et Politique, Indépendance et Coopération* no. 3 (1968): 893–908.

418. De Lauwe, Paul-Henry Chombart. *Images de la femme dans la société.* Recherche Internationale sous la Direction de Paul-Henry Chombart de Lauwe. Paris: Editions Ouvrières, 1964.

419. Demeerseman, A. 'La route féminine.' *Revue de l' Institut des Belles Lettres Arabes* 5 (1942): 329–346.

420. Deonna, Laurence. *Moyen Orient: Femmes de combat, de la terre et du sable.* Genève: Editions Labor et Fides, 1970.

421. Desanti, Dominique. 'No more Veils.' *Atlas* 9 (1965): 91–93.

422. Dixon, Ruth B. 'The Roles of Rural Women: Female

Seclusion, Economic Production and Reproductive Choice.' *Resources for the Future*. Paper presented at the Conference on Population Policy from the Socio-Economic Perspective, Washington, D.C., 1975.

423. Dodd, Peter. 'The Effect of Religious Affiliation on Women's Role in Middle Eastern Arab Society.' Paper presented at the 8th World Congress of Sociology, Session on Sex-Roles and Society, Toronto, 1974. (Also in *Journal of Comparative Family Study* 5, 2 (1974):117–129.)

424. Dodd, Peter. 'Family Honor and the Forces of Change in Arab Society.' Paper presented at the 4th Annual Meeting of the Middle East Studies Association, Columbus, Ohio, 4 Nov., 1970. (Also in *International Journal of Middle East Studies* 4, 1 (1975): 40–54.)

425. Dodd, Peter. 'Women Students in Higher Education.' American University of Beirut, Lebanon, 1972.

426. Dostal, W. 'Zum Problem der Mädchenbeschneidung in Arabien.' *Wiener Völkerkundliche Mitteilungen* no. 6 (1959):83–89.

427. Duverger, Maurice. *La participation des femmes à la vie politique*. Paris: Presses Blondin, 1955.

428. Eekelaar, J.M., Davis, J.L.R. and Webb, P.R.H. 'The Dissolution of Originally Polygamous Marriages.' *International and Comparative Law Quarterly* 15 (1966):1181–1189.

429. Elwan, Shwikar. *The Status of Women in the Arab World*. New York: Arab League Information Center, 1974.

430. Ergunduz, Mirgun. 'The Role of Women in Development with Special Reference to the Middle East.' M.A. thesis, American University of Beirut, Lebanon, 1969.

431. El-Eteify, Gamal. 'The Legal Status of Women in Arab Countries and its Impact on their Participation in National Development.' Paper presented at the Seminar on Arab Women in National Development, sponsored by UNICEF, Arab League and Arab

States Adult Functional Literacy Center, Cairo, 24–30 Sept., 1972.

432. Evans-Pritchard, Edward E. *The Position of Women in Primitive Societies and Other Essays in Social Anthropology.* London: Faber and Faber, 1965.

433. Faffler, Irene. 'A Cross-Cultural Study of the Task-Oriented Small Group in the Middle East.' Ph.D. dissertation, University of Minnesota, 1971.

434. Fahmi, Aisha A. and Taha, H.M. 'Arab Women in Labor Legislations.' Paper presented at the Seminar on Arab Women in National Development, sponsored by UNICEF, Arab League and Arab States Adult Functional Literacy Center, Cairo, 24–30 Sept., 1972.

435. Fahmi, Noha, and Ramzi, Nahed. 'Women's Role in Social Development.' Paper presented at the Afro-Arab Parliamentary Congress, Cairo, Egypt, May 1974.

436. Farber, M.A. 'Women Gaining Ground in Arab Nations.' *New York Times,* 22 Oct., 1974.

437. Farrag, Osman, L. 'Arab Women and National Development.' *Assignment Children* 23 (July–Sept. 1973): 87–97.

438. Al-Faruqi, Lamia. 'Prescription for a Muslim Women's Movement.' Paper presented at the 9th International Congress of Anthropological and Ethnological Sciences, Chicago, Ill., Aug.–Sept. 1973.

439. Federal Republic of Germany. Federal Ministry of Economic Cooperation. *Report on Improving the Status of Women in Developing Countries, 1978.* (Résumé in *WIN News* 4, 3 (Summer 1978):9–10.)

440. 'La femme à la recherche d'elle-même.' Papers presented at the Semaine de la Pensée Marxiste de Lyon, 4–10 Feb., 1965. Paris: La Palatine, 1965.

441. 'La femme et la législation des pays Arabes à la lumière des accords internationaux.' Recommandations au Séminaire de Beyrouth, 27–31 May, 1974. *Travaux et Jours* 52 (July–Sept. 1974):71–76.

442. Fergany, Nader. 'Arab Women and National Development: a Demographic Background.' Paper presented

at the Seminar on Arab Women in National Development, sponsored by UNICEF, Arab League and Arab States Adult Functional Literacy Center, Cairo, Egypt, 24–30 Sept., 1972.

443. Fernea, Elizabeth. 'The Dynamics of Change in the Status of Middle Eastern Women.' Paper presented at the Symposium of Near Eastern Women Through the Ages, Berkeley, University of California, 1975.

444. Fernea, Elizabeth W. and Bezirgan, Basima, eds. 'Women's World Female Festivals.' Paper presented at the 9th Annual Meeting of the Middle East Studies Association, Louisville, Ky., 19–22 Nov., 1975.

445. Fernea, Elizabeth W. and Bezirgan, Basima, eds. *Middle Eastern Muslim Women Speak*. Austin: University of Texas Press, 1977.

446. Fernea, E. and Joseph, S. 'A Brief Commentary and Report on the Roundtable and Panels on Women's Roles Held at the 1975 MESA Meeting.' *Middle East Studies Association Bulletin* 10, 2 (May 1976): 20–23.

447. Fernea, E. and Qattan, Basima. *Women's Organizations and Leaders Directory*, 1975–1976. Austin: University of Texas Press, 1977.

448. Fluehr-Lobban, Carolyn. 'National Liberation in Africa and the Arab World: a Comparative View of Women's Political Participation.' Paper prepared for the Wellesley Conference on Women and Development, Wellesley College, Mass., 2–6 June, 1976.

449. Fluehr-Lobban, Carolyn. 'Some Suggestions Regarding the Political Mobilization of Women in the Arab World.' Paper prepared for the Workshop on the Status and Role of Women in Contemporary Muslim Societies, Center for the Study of World Religions, Harvard University, 19 Apr., 1975.

450. Fluehr-Lobban, Carolyn. 'Women and National Liberation in the Arab World.' Paper presented at the 8th Annual Convention of Arab-American University Graduates, Chicago, 17–19 Oct., 1975.

451. Fox, Greer Litton and Merriam, K.H., eds. Prospectus for 'The Emergence of the Modern Woman in the Middle East: Studies in Emancipation.'

452. 'Fringe Benefits.' *Time* 24 Aug., 1959, p. 24.

453. Fuleihan, Louise. 'The Arab Women's Congress, Cairo, Egypt, 1944.' *Muslim World* 35 (1945): 316–323.

454. Galenson, Marjorie. *Women and Work: an International Comparison*. Ithaca, N.Y.: Cornell University Press, 1973.

455. Galtier, F. *Le mariage: discipline orientale et discipline occidentale*. Beirut: Université Saint Joseph de Beyrouth, Faculté de Théologie, Publications du 75ème Anniversaire, 1950.

456. Germanus, Julius. 'The Trend of Contemporary Arabic Literature; the Role of Women in Arabic Literature.' *Islamic Quarterly* 4, 3 (Oct. 1957):114–122.

457. El-Ghonemy, M. Riad. 'Integrated Rural Development and the Interrelationships of Population Factors and Status of Women. The Concept of Integrated Rural Development.' Paper presented at the Seminar on the Role of Women in Integrated Rural Development with Emphasis on Population Problems, Cairo, Egypt, 26 Oct.–3 Nov., 1974.

458. Giele, Janet Z. and Smock, Audrey C. *Women and Society in International and Comparative Perspective*. New York: Wiley-Interscience, 1977.

459. Giffen, Lois Anita. *Theory of Profane Love Among the Arabs: the Development of the Genre*. New York: New York University Press, 1971.

460. Gabriel, Giuseppe, *I tempi, la vita e il canzoniere della poetessa araba al-Ḥansâ*. Roma: Istituto per l'Oriente, 1944.

461. Goldziher, Ignaz. 'Women in the Ḥadīth Literature' in *Muslim Studies*, ed. S.M. Stern, vol. II (1971).

462. Goody, Jack R. and Tambiah, S.J. *Bridewealth and Dowry*. London: Cambridge University Press, 1974.

463. Graziani, J. 'The Momentum of the Feminist Movement in the Arab World.' *Middle East Review* 7, 2 (1974):26–33.

464. Grimal, Pierre, ed. *Histoire Mondiale de la Femme*, 4 Vols. Paris: Nouvelle Librairie de France, 1967.
465. Gruyther, L. 'Mixed Marriages.' *Journal of Comparative Legislation and International Law* II (1929):34-41.
466. Haddad, William. 'The Legal Provisions Governing the Status of Women in Some Arab Countries.' *Population Bulletin of the United Nations Economic Commission for Western Asia* no. 14 (June 1977): 26-46.
467. Al-Haj, Fawzi M. 'Rural Women as Participants and Recipients in Integrated Rural Development.' Paper presented at the Seminar on the Role of Women in Integrated Rural Development with Emphasis on Population Problems, Cairo, Egypt, 26 Oct.-3 Nov., 1974.
468. Hajjar, Raja. 'The Preparation of Arab Women for Scientific and Technological Development.' Paper, Beirut, Lebanon.
469. Halimi, Gisèle. *La cause des femmes. Propos recueillis par Marie Cardinal.* Paris: B. Grasset, 1973.
470. Al-Hamdani, M. and Abu-Laban, B. 'Game Involvement and Sex Role Socialization in Arab Children.' *International Journal of Comparative Sociology* 12 (1971):182-191.
471. Hanania, Edith. 'A Survey of the Development of Higher Education for Women in the Arab World.' Research Project in Progress sponsored by the Institute for Women's Studies in the Arab World, Beirut University College, Beirut, Lebanon.
472. Harry, Myriam. 'La nouvelle genération féminine en Orient.' *Annales Politiques et Littéraires* 4, 1 (1925):5-6.
473. Hickey, Margaret. 'Woman's Role in a Changing World.' Address delivered at the Centennial Public Affairs Lecture, American University of Beirut, Beirut, 18 Oct., 1966.
474. Hilal, Jamil. 'Father's Brother's Daughter Marriage in Arab Communities: a Problem for Sociological Explanation.' *Middle East Forum* 46,4 (1972) :73-84.
475. Hilal, Jamil. 'The Management of Male Dominance in

"Traditional" Arab Culture: a Tentative Model.' *Civilization* 21, 1 (1971): 85–95.

476. Hillary, Nyall St. Joseph. 'The Nightmare of Female Circumcision.' *Monday Morning*, 28 May–3 June, 1973, pp. 32–35.

477. Hourani, Furugh. 'Uncertain Equality.' *Times* (London), 8 March 1968.

478. Hume-Griffith, M.E. *Behind the Veil in Persia and Turkish Arabia*, London: Seeley, 1909.

479. Hussein, Aziza. 'Changing Conditions of Women and its Effect on Children.' *Journal of the American Medical Women's Association* 21, 9 (1966).

480. Hussein, Aziza. 'Role of Women in the Arab World.' Paper delivered at the Workshop of WFUNA/ ISMUN on Human Roles of Women in Society and in Development, Sweden, 14–18 Aug., 1974.

481. Huston, Perdita. *Third World Women Speak out: Interviews in Six Countries on Change, Development and Basic Needs*. New York: Praeger, 1979.

482. Ibn Hazm, Abu Muhammad Ali Ibn Muhammad Ibn Said. *The Ring of the Dove: a Treatise on the Art and Practice of Arab Love*. Translated by A.J. Arberry. London: Luzac, 1953.

483. Iglitzin, Lynne B. *Women in the World: a Comparative Study*. Studies in Comparative Politics, no. 6. Santa Barbara, Calif.: ABC-Clio, 1976.

484. 'Il V congresso dell'unione femminile araba a Beirut.' (Fifth Congress of the Arab Women's Union in Beirut.) *Oriente Moderno* 14, 6 (1934): 280–281.

485. ILO. *Employment and Vocational Training for Women in the Arab Countries* (ETF/AR/4, 26 Sept., 1969). Paper presented at the UNESCO Expert Meeting on the Equality of Access of Girls and Women to Technical and Vocational Education in the Arab Countries, Kuwait, 1–7 Nov., 1969.

486. ILO. 'Summary of ILO Standards Relating to Women's Employment.' Paper presented at the Seminar on the Role of Women in Integrated Rural Development with Emphasis on Population Problems, Cairo, Egypt, 26 Oct.–3 Nov., 1974.

487. ILO. 'Women Workers in the Third World and the ILO Contribution' (ILO/W/2/1974). Geneva, 1974.

488. Ingrams, Doreen. *A Time in Arabia.* London: John Murray, 1970.

489. Institute for Women's Studies in the Arab World, Beirut University College, Lebanon. *Al-Raida*, 1976– , quarterly. (Newsletter reporting recent research and up-to-date information about women in the Arab World. No. 1, May 1976; No. 2, Sept. 1977; No. 3, Feb. 1978; then quarterly.)

490. International Bank for Reconstruction and Development. *Integrating Women into Development.* Washington, D.C.: International Bank for Reconstruction and Development, 1975.

491. International Federation of Business and Professional Women. *Study of the Role of Women: their Activities and Organizations in Lebanon, Egypt, Iraq, Syria and Jordan.* New York: International Federation of Business and Professional Women, 1956.

492. Ismail, Souad Khalil. 'Women's Education in the Arab Countries.' *L'Education Nouvelle* (UNESCO) (April 1975).

493. Al-Isa, M. 'The First Regional Conference for Women in the Arab Gulf.' *Journal of Gulf and Arabian Peninsula Studies* 1, 3 (July 1975):225–30.

494. *Isis: International Bulletin*, 1976– , quarterly. ('Isis is coordinating the International Feminist Network.') Isis Collective, Via della Pelliccia 31, 00153 Rome, Italy and Case Postale 301, 1227 Carouge/Geneva, Switzerland.

495. Izzeddine, Randa. 'Role Conflict in Female College Students, Sex Roles.' M.A. thesis, American University of Beirut, Lebanon, 1974.

496. Jabri, Pearl. *Arab Women in Love.* Beirut: Imprimerie Systeco, n.d.

497. Jacob, J.A. 'Maximes et proverbes populaires arabes: la famille.' *Mélanges de l'Institut Dominicain d'Etudes Orientales du Caire* (MIDEO) 7 (1962): 35–80.

498. Jacobs, Sue Ellen. *Women in Perspective: a Guide for*

Cross Cultural Studies. Chicago: University of Chicago Press, 1974.

499. Jamali, Sarah Fadhel. 'Raising the Veil.' *Asia* (Aug. 1935):494–497.

500. Jamous, R. 'Réflexions sur la segmentarité et le mariage arabe.' *Annales Marocaines de Sociologie,* 1969.

501. Jansen, Michael Elin. 'Nursing in the Arab East.' *Aramco World Magazine* Mar./Apr. 1974, pp. 14–23.

502. Jessup, Henry Harris. *The Women of the Arabs.* New York: Dodd and Mead, n.d.

503. Johnston, Margaret L. 'What the Faith of a Moslem Woman Lacks.' *Muslim World* 9 (1916):340–346.

504. Jomier, J. 'Un livre récent sur la femme.' *Mélanges de l'Institut Dominicain d'Etudes Orientales du Caire* (MIDEO) 1 (1954):150–162.

505. Joyce, Thomas A., ed. *Women of All Nations: a Record of their Characteristics, Habits, Manners, Customs and Influence,* 4 Vols. Ann Arbor, Mich.: Finch Press, 1974. (Reprint of 1915 edition.)

506. Katz, Naomi and Milton, Nancy. *Fragment from a Lost Diary and other Stories: Women of Asia, Africa and Latin America.* New York: Pantheon, 1973.

507. Katz, N. and Milton, N., eds. *Women of the Third World.* London: Gollancz, 1976.

508. Keddie, Nikki. 'Methodological Problems in the Study of Middle Eastern Women.' Paper presented at the Wellesley Conference on Women and Development, Wellesley College, Mass., 2–6 June, 1976.

509. Keddie, Nikki. 'Problems in the Study of Middle Eastern Women.' *International Journal of Middle East Studies* 10 (1979):225–240.

510. Kesler, Suad Wakim. 'Values of Women College Students in the Arab Middle East.' Ph.D. dissertation, Cornell University, 1965.

511. Keyser, J. 'The Middle Eastern Case: Is there a Marriage Rule?' *Ethnology* 13, 3 (1974):293–309.

512. Al-Khalidi, Anbara. 'Woman's Role in Arab Society.' *Islamic Review* 37 (Nov. 1949):19–22.

513. Khalil, Rasmiya. 'Problem Impeding Women Participation in National Development.' Paper presented

C

in a Seminar on Arab Women in National Development, sponsored by UNICEF, Arab League and Arab States Adult Functional Literacy Center, Cairo, Egypt, 24–30 Sept., 1972.

514. El-Khayyat, Ghitta. 'A Study on the Evolutionary, Medical and Psychological Aspects of Female Employment in a Third World Country.' Paper presented at the Seminar on Women in Development, Mexico City, Mexico, 16–18 June, 1975.

515. Khuda Bakhsh, Salahuddin. *Marriage and Family Life Among the Arabs*, 2nd edn. Lahore: Orientalia, 1953.

516. Khuri, Fuad I. 'Father's Brother's Daughter Marriage Reconsidered: a Middle Eastern Practice that Nullifies the Effects of Marriage on the Intensity of Family Relationships.' *Man: Journal of the Royal Anthropological Institute* (Dec. 1970):597–610.

517. Klein, Viola. *The Feminine Character: History of an Ideology*. London: Routledge and Kegan Paul, 1971.

518. Klein, Viola. *Women Workers: Working Hours and Services: a Survey in 21 Countries*. Paris: Organization for Economic Cooperation and Development, 1965.

519. Kupinsky, Stanley, ed. *The Fertility of Working Women*. New York: Praeger, 1977.

520. Laidlaw, R.G.B. 'Some Reflections on Nursing in the Middle East.' *Arab World* 37 (Oct. 1958):23–24.

521. Lamsa, George M. *The Secret of the Near East: Slavery of Women, Social, Religious and Economic Life in the Near East*. Philadelphia: Ideal Press, 1923.

522. Larsen, P. Address of the UNICEF Representative at the Opening of the Seminar on the Role of Women in Integrated Rural Development with Particular Emphasis on Population Problems. Cairo, Egypt, 26 Oct.–3 Nov., 1974.

523. Layson, H. 'The Religious Condition of Oriental Women.' *Actes du IIIe Congrès International du Christianisme Liberal et Progressif, Genève* (1906): 110–119.

524. Legassick, T. 'Ihsan Abd El Quddus: Chief Exponent of Female Arab Attitudes.' *Middle East* 8, 6 (Nov.–Dec. 1968):24–26.

525. Lehrman, Hal. 'Battle of the Veil.' *New York Times Magazine* 13 July, 1958, pp. 14–18.

526. Lemanski, Witold. *Moeurs arabes (Scènes vécues)*. Paris: Albin Michel, n.d.

527. Lesley, Blanche. 'The Seven Veils of Islam.' *Sunday Times Magazine* (London), Nov. 1970, pp. 34–55.

528. Leslie, Doris. *The Desert Queen*. London: Heinemann, 1972.

529. Lichtenstadter, Ilse. *Women of the Aiyam Al-Arab: a Study of Female Life During Warfare in Pre-Islamic Arabia*. London: Royal Asiatic Society, 1935.

530. Lockyer, Herbert. *The Women of the Bible: the Life and Times of all the Women of the Bible*. Grand Rapids, Mich.: Zondervan, 1967.

531. Lofts, Norah (Robinson). *Women in the Old Testament: Twenty Psychological Portraits*. New York: Macmillan, 1949.

532. Loya, Arieh. 'Poetry as a Social Document: the Social Position of the Arab Woman as Reflected in the Poetry of Nizar Qabbani.' *Muslim World* 63, 1 (Jan. 1973):39–52. (Also in *International Journal of Middle East Studies* 6 (Oct. 1975):481–94.)

533. MacDonald-Fahey, Patricia. 'Women's Liberation—Arab Style.' *Wall Street Journal*, 11 July, 1975.

534. Makarius, Raoul. 'Le mariage des cousins parallèls chez les Arabes.' *Extrait des Actes du VI Congrés International des Sciences Anthropologiques et Ethnologiques*. Paris, n.d.

535. Marmorstein, Emile. 'The Veil in Judaism and Islam.' *Journal of Jewish Studies* 5, 2 (1954):1–11.

536. Al Masry, Youssef. *Le drame sexuel de la femme dans l'Orient Arabe*. Paris: Laffont, 1962.

537. Mathews, Basil. 'Woman in the Near East.' *Muslim World* 9 (1919):240–246.

538. Matthiasson, Carolyn J., ed. *Many Sisters: Women in Cross-Cultural Perspective*. New York: Free Press, 1974.

539. Mazumdar, V., ed. *Role of Rural Women in Development*. New Delhi: Allied Publishers, 1978.

540. McGrath, Patricia. 'Women: Education is the Key.' *U.N. Development Forum*, Dec. 1976, p. 8.

541. Melconian, Marlene. 'Arab Women: in Hot Pursuit of a Feminist-Oriented Economy.' *Arab Economist*, Aug. 1975, pp. 18–26.

542. Melikian, Levon. 'The Dethronement of the Father.' *Middle East Forum* 36, 1 (Jan. 1960):23–26.

543. Melikian, L.H. and Prothro, E. 'Sexual Behavior of University Students in the Arab Near East.' *Journal of Abnormal and Social Psychology* 49 (1954): 59–64.

544. Mernissi, Fatima. 'Clarification and Misunderstandings Existing Between Industrialization, Modernization and Development of Resources and Human Potential.' Paper presented at the Seminar on Women in Development, Mexico City, 16–18 June, 1975.

545. Mernissi, Fatima. 'Women, Saints and Sanctuaries'. *Signs: Journal of Women in Culture and Society* 3, 1 (Autumn 1977):101–112.

546. Miller, Kaity and Mendelsohn, Micaela. 'Education and the Participation of Women in World Development: a Brief Survey.' Washington: Women's Equity Action League, 1975.

547. Minturn, L. and Hambert, W.W. *Mothers of Six Cultures: Antecedents of Child Rearing*. New York: John Wiley, 1964.

548. Mirshak, Myra. 'Six Arab Countries to Form Unified Women's Organization.' *Daily Star*, 18 Jan., 1975, p. 7.

549. Mogannam, Mathilde. *The Arab Woman*. London: Herbert Joseph, 1937.

550. Mohsen, A. *et al.* 'Arab Women Still the Underdog.' *Middle East* no. 41 (Mar. 1978):61–72.

551. Mohsen, Safia. 'The Legal Status of Women Among Awlad Ali.' *Anthropological Quarterly* 40 (1967): 153–166.

552. Morton, H.V. *Women of the Bible*. New York: Dodd, 1950.

553. Muhyi, Ibrahim Abdulla. 'Women in the Arab Middle East.' *Journal of Social Issues* 15, 3 (1959):45–57.
554. Mulliken, Frances and Salts, Margaret. *Women of Destiny in the Bible*. Independence, Mo.: Herald House, 1978.
555. Murphy, Robert F. 'Social Distance and the Veil.' *American Anthropologist* 66 (1964):1257–1274.
556. Mustaffa-Kedah, Omar. 'The Education of Women in the Arab States.' *Literacy Discussion* 6, 4 (Winter 1975–76):119–139.
557. Mustaffa-Kedah, Omar. 'Towards a Rational Education for Women in the Arab World.' International Institute for Adult Literacy Methods, Tehran, Iran, 1976.
558. Nahas, K. 'The Family in the Arab World.' *Marriage and Family Living* 16 (1954):293–300.
559. Najjar, Mona. 'The Changing Role of Rural Women.' M.A. thesis, American University of Beirut, Lebanon, 1972.
560. Najmun Nisa, Begum. 'Arab Attitude Towards Women, up to the End of the 3rd Century of Hijra, mainly as Shown by the 'Iqd of Ibn 'Abd Rabbihi'. *Proceedings the All-Pakistan History Conference* I (1951): 44–59.
561. Naser, Abdallah Omar. 'The Educational Philosophy of Certain Prospective American and Arab Women Teachers.' Ph.D. dissertation, University of Florida, 1966.
562. *Nederlands-Arabische Kring 1955–1965: Eight Studies Marking its First Decade*. Leiden: E.J. Brill, 1966. (Chapter by G.W. Drewes on 'The Beginning of the Emancipation of Women in the Arab World'.)
563. Nelson, Cynthia. 'Between Social Worlds: the Case of Nomadic Women.' Paper, 1972.
564. Nelson, Cynthia. 'Public and Private Politics: Women in the Middle Eastern World.' *American Ethnologist* 1, 3 (Aug. 1974):551–64.
565. Nelson, Cynthia. 'Seclusion and Emancipation: Changing Roles of Man and Woman in the Middle East.' Paper, American University of Cairo, 1972.
566. Nelson, Cynthia. ed. *The Desert and the Sown: Nomads*

in the Greater Society. Berkeley: University of California, Institute of International Studies, 1973.

567. Newsland, Kathleen. *Women in Politics: a Global Review.* Washington, D.C.: Worldwatch Institute, 1975.

568. O'Barr, Jean F. *The Changing Roles of Women in Developing Countries.* Durham, N.C.: Duke University, Comparative Area Studies Program, June 1975.

569. O'Barr, Jean F. *Third World Women: Factors in their Changing Status.* Durham, N.C.: Duke University, Center for International Studies, Oct. 1976.

570. Oden, R.A. 'The Persistence of Canaanite Religion.' *Biblical Archeologist* 39 (Mar. 1976):31–36.

571. 'Opinions sur le mariage mixte.' *Revue de Presse* 79 (1963).

572. 'Ordre du jour du comité éxecutif du Congrès de l'Union Féministe Orientale.' *En Terre D'Islam* no. 45 (1931):120–124.

573. Palmer, Ingrid. 'The Basic Needs Approach to the Integration of Rural Women in Development: Conditions for Success.' n.d. (Mimeographed.)

574. Paret, R. *Zur Frauenfrage in der arabisch–islamischen Welt.* (About Emancipation of Women in the Writings of Mohammad Rashid Rida, Lebanon; Nazira Zain Al-Din, Lebanon; and Tahir Al-Haddad, Tunis.) Stuttgart: Kohlhammer, 1934.

575. Partington, M. 'Polygamous Marriages—is a "Wife" a Wife.' *International and Comparative Law Quarterly* 16 (1967):805–808.

576. Patai, Raphael. *The Arab Mind.* New York: Charles Scribner's Sons, 1973.

577. Patai, Raphael. 'Cousin Right in Middle Eastern Marriages.' *Southwestern Journal of Anthropology* 2 (Winter 1955).

578. Patai, Raphael. *Women in the Modern World.* New York: Free Press, 1967.

579. Penzer, Norman Mosley. *The Harem: an Account of the Institution as it Existed in the Palace of the Turkish Sultans, with a History of the Grand*

Seraglio from its Foundation to the Present Time.
London: Harrap, 1936.

580. Pestalozza, Uberto. *L'éternel féminin dans la religion méditerranéenne.* Traduction et Préface de Marcel de Corte. Bruxelles: Berchem, Latomus, 1965.

581. Peters, Emrys. 'Consequences of the Segregation of the Sexes Among the Arabs.' Paper presented at the Mediterranean Social Science Council Conference, Athens, 1966.

582. Peters, Emrys. 'Sex Differentiation in Two Arab Communities.' Paper, University of Manchester, Department of Anthropology, 1967. (Mimeographed.)

583. Philipp, T. 'Women in the Historical Perspective of an Early Arab Modernist (Gurgi Zaidan).' *Die Welt des Islams* 18, 1–2 (1977):65–83.

584. Piesse, Louis. 'La femme arabe.' *La Revue de l'Afrique Française* (1887).

585. Al-Qazzaz, A. 'Current Status of Research on Woman in the Arab World.' *Middle Eastern Studies* 14 (Oct. 1978):372–380.

586. Smith, William R. *Kinship and Marriage in Early Arabia.* London: Adam and Charles Black, 1903.

587. Rohlich-Leavitt, Ruby, ed. *Women Cross-Culturally: Change and Challenge.* The Hague: Mouton, 1975.

588. Rosaldo, M. and Lamphere, L. *Women, Culture and Society.* Stanford, Calif.: Stanford University, 1974.

589. Rosenfeld, Henry. 'On Determinants of the Status of Arab Village Women.' *Man* 60 (May 1960):66–70.

590. Royere, Jean. *Harems et pied dorés.* Paris, Vautier, 1970.

591. Rubeiz, Ghassan. 'Adjustment of Middle Eastern Women on Beirut University College Campus.' (Résumé of no. 592.) Paper presented at the University of Tennessee, School of Social Work, Knoxville, Tenn., 1977.

592. Rubeiz, Ghassan. 'Adjustment of Women Students in an Arab College: Beirut University College.' Research project sponsored by the Institute for Women's Studies in the Arab World, Beirut University College, Lebanon, 1975.

593. Rubeiz, Ghassan. 'Dating in a Middle Eastern Campus.' Research project sponsored by the Institute for Women's Studies in the Arab World, Beirut University College, Lebanon, 1977. *Journal of Comparative Family Studies* (Spring 1979).

594. Saab, Edouard. 'Statut et conditions de la femme orientale.' *Action Proche-Orient* 22 (May 1964): 46–48.

595. Sadawi, Nawal, Mernissi, F. and Vajrathon, M. 'A Critical Look at the Wellesley Conference.' *Quest: a Feminist Quarterly*, 4, 2 (Winter 1978): 101–108.

596. Safilios-Rothschild, Constantina. 'A Cross-Cultural Examination of Women's Marital, Educational and Occupational Options.' *Acta Sociologica* 14 (1971): 86–113.

597. Safilios-Rothschild, Constantina. 'The Current Status of Women Cross-Culturally: Change and Persisting Barriers.' *Theological Studies* 36 (1975):577–604.

598. Safilios-Rothschild, Constantina. 'Social Indicators of the Status of Women.' Paper commissioned by the United Nations Secretariat for International Women's Year, n.d.

599. Es-Said, Nimra (Nimra Tannous). 'Women and Development in some Countries of the Near East.' M.A. thesis, Institute of Social Sciences, The Hague, Netherlands, 1964.

600. Salman, Sylvia. 'Sex and Personality.' B.A. thesis, American University of Beirut, Lebanon, 1965.

601. Samaan, N.J. 'La femme arabe au seuil de la liberté.' *Croissance des Jeunes Nations* 23 (June/July 1973): 29–32.

602. El-Sanabary, Nagat. 'The Education of Women in the Arab States: Achievements and Problems 1950–1970.' Paper presented at the 8th Annual Meeting of the Middle East Studies Association, Boston, 6–9 Nov., 1974. (Also presented at the Symposium of Near Eastern Women Through the Ages, Berkeley, Calif., 1975.)

603. El-Sanabary, Nagat. 'Comparative Study of Disparities of Educational Opportunities for Women in the

Arab States.' Ph.D. dissertation, University of California, Berkeley, 1973.

604. El-Sanabary, Nagat. 'Women's Education—Remarkable Progress, but Problems Remain.' *American Friends of the Middle East Report*, July 1975, pp. 1–8.

605. Sayegh, Rosemary. 'The Changing Life of Arab Women.' *Mid-East* 8, 6 (1968): 19–23.

606. Schlegel, Alice. *Male Dominance and Female Autonomy: Domestic Authority in Matrilineal Societies.* New Haven, Conn.: Hraf Press, 1972.

607. Schneider, Jane. 'Of Vigilance and Virgins: Honor, Shame and Access to Resources in Mediterranean Societies.' *Ethnology* 10, 1 (1971): 1–24.

608. Seilbert, Ilse. *Women in the Ancient Near East.* London: G. Prior Associated Publishers, 1975.

609. Seklani, Mahmoud. 'La fécondité dans les pays arabes.' *Population* 15 (1960): 831–856.

610. Senfeld, Henry. 'On Determinants of the Status of Arab Village Women.' *Man* 60 (1960): 66–70.

611. 'Sex Roles in Cross-Cultural Perspectives.' *American Ethnologist* 2, 4 (1975). (Special Issue.)

612. Shafie, Erfan and Bassyouni, A. 'The Role of Women in Economic and Social Development.' *Proceedings of the Afro-Arab Interparliamentary Women's Conference.* Cairo, Egypt, May 1974.

613. 'Shedding the Veil.' *Newsweek*, 25 Oct., 1971, pp. 59–60.

614. Shilling, Nancy A. (Hunter). 'The Political and Social Roles of Arab Women: a Study in Conflict.' Paper presented at the 8th Annual Meeting of the Middle East Studies Association, Boston, 6–9 Nov., 1974.

615. Smith, Page. *Daughters of the Promised Land.* Boston: Little, Brown, 1970.

616. Smith, William Robertson. *Kinship and Marriage in Early Arabia,* 2nd edn. New Jersey: Humanities Press, 1973.

617. Singletary, James D. 'Enhancing the Role of Women in Developing Countries.' *Report of the AdHoc Committee on Education and Human Resources,* Technical Assistance Bureau, Agency for International Development, Feb. 1973.

618. Sims, Ottley Shaw. 'Honor and Modesty in the Middle East.' M.A. thesis, submitted in partial fulfillment of the requirements for a Master's Degree, Middle East Area Studies, American University of Beirut, Lebanon, 1973.

619. Shukri, Ahmed. *Muhammedan Law of Marriage and Divorce.* New York: AMS Press, 1917.

620. Smock, Audrey C. and Giele, J. *Women and Society: an International and Comparative Perspective.* New York: Wiley-Interscience, 1977.

621. 'Social Life and the Women of the Near East.' *Muslim World* 25 (1935):236–241.

622. Spencer, Robert F. 'The Arabian Matriarchate: an Old Controversy.' *Southwestern Journal of Anthropology* 8, 4 (1952):478–502.

623. Stoltzfus, W.A. 'A Plan for Higher Education of Women.' Beirut College for Women, Lebanon, 1950.

624. Tabesh, Intisar. 'Women in Arabic Press.' B.A. thesis, American University of Beirut, Lebanon, 1953.

625. Technical Assistance Information Clearing House (TAICH). Subcommittee on Women in Development. *Criteria for Evaluation of Development Projects Involving Women.* New York: TAICH, Dec. 1975.

626. al-Talib, N. 'Status of Woman in Islam.' *Islamic Literature* 15, 6 (1969):57–64.

627. Tannous, Nimra (Es-Said, Nimra Tannous). *Women— the Scapegoat of Society.* Swansea: Swansea University College, 1955.

628. Tapper, Nancy. 'The Role of Women in Selected Pastoral Islamic Society.' M.A. thesis in Philosophy, University of London, 1968.

629. Tarazi, M.F. 'Attitude Toward Feminism Among Arab Women as Related to their Need for Achievement, Sex Role Preference and Vocational Choice.' M.A. thesis, American University of Beirut, Lebanon, 1972.

630. Tillion, Germaine. 'Les femmes et le voile dans la civilisation méditerranéenne.' *Etudes Maghrébines: Mélanges Charles-André Julien* (1964):25–38.

631. Tillion, Germaine. 'Implications économiques du mariage.' *Littérature Orale Arabo-Berbere* no. 6–7 (1973–1974):185–188.

632. Tinker, Irene. 'The Adverse Impact of Development on Women.' Paper presented at the Comparative Area Studies Conference, Duke University, Durham, N.C., 1975.

633. Tomeh, Aida. 'Birth Order, Club Membership and Mass Media Exposure.' *Journal of Marriage and the Family* (Feb. 1976):151–164.

634. Tomeh, Aida. 'Birth Order and Friendship Associations.' *Journal of Marriage and the Family* 32, 3 (Aug. 1970):360–369.

635. Tomeh, Aida. 'Birth Order and Dependence Patterns of College Students in Lebanon.' *Journal of Marriage and the Family* (May 1972):361–374.

636. Tomeh, Aida. 'Birth Order and Kinship Affiliation.' *Journal of Marriage and the Family* (Feb. 1969):19–26.

637. Tomeh, Aida. 'Cross-Cultural Differences in the Structure of Moral Values: a Factorial Analysis.' *International Journal of Comparative Sociology* 11, 1 (Mar. 1970):18–33.

638. Tomeh, Aida. *The Family and Sex Roles*. Toronto: Holt, Rinehart and Winston of Canada, 1975.

639. Tomeh, Aida. 'The Impact of Reference Groups on the Educational and Occupational Aspirations of Women College Students.' *Journal of Marriage and the Family* 30, 1 (1968):102–110.

640. Tomeh, Aida. 'Reference-group Supports Among Middle Eastern College Students.' *Journal of Marriage and the Family* 32, 1 (Feb. 1970):156–166.

641. Al-Torki, Soraya. 'Men–Women Relationship in Arab Societies: a Study of the Economic and Political Conditions of the Status of Women.' Unpublished research proposal, 1973.

642. Tuckwell, Sue and Moore, Kate. *We Women* (Kit of Pamphlets on Women in Many Countries Including Africa and Arabia). Australian Council for Overseas Education, P.O. Box 1562, Canberra City, ACT 2601, Australia.

643. El-Turki, Ahmed Mohamed Ali. 'Femmes privilégiées et féminines dans le système théologique et juridique d'Ibn Hazm.' *Studia Islamica* 47 (1978):25–82.

644. 'Women and Out-of-School Education in Arab Countries.' Paper presented at the Seminar on Arab Women in National Development sponsored by UNICEF, Arab League and Arab States Adult Functional Literacy Center, Cairo, Egypt, 24–30 Sept., 1972.

645. Turton, Godfrey. *The Syrian Princesses: The Women Who Ruled Rome, A.D. 193–235*. London: Cassell, 1974.

646. UNESCO. 'Access of Girls to Education in Arab States.' *UNESCO Chronicle* 10 (May 1964):173.

647. UNESCO. 'Access of Women to Out of School Education—Arab States' (396/U55a, ED/207. ED/MD/1). Paris.

648. UNESCO. 'Report on the Relationship between Educational Opportunities and Employment Opportunities for Women' (1975/ED, 74/W5–56). Paris.

649. UNESCO. 'Comparative Study on Access of Girls and Women to Technical and Vocational Education' (ED/MD/3), 1968.

650. UNESCO. 'General Progress Report of the Executive Director. Programme Developments in the Eastern Mediterranean. Report on Women and Girls in National Development' (E/ICEF/616/Add. 3/Annex). Geneva, 1972.

651. UNESCO. 'International Women's Year, 1975.' *UNESCO Features* (No. 676/677/678). (Includes Egypt and Lebanon among others.)

652. UNESCO. 'Meeting of Experts on the Access of Girls to School Education in the Arab States' (ED/207). Algiers, 6–16 Apr., 1964.

653. UNESCO. 'Meeting of Experts on the Access of Girls and Women to Technical and Vocational Education in the Arab States' (ED/MD/9). Kuwait, 1–7 Nov., 1969. Paris, 1970.

654. UNESCO. 'New Women in the Arab World.' *UNESCO Information Bulletin* 19 (Nov. 1964).

655. UNESCO. Commission on the Status of Women. 'The United Nations Decade for Women: Equality, Development and Peace 1976–1985. Report of the Commission on the Status of Arab Women' (E/CN. 6/597). Geneva, Aug. 1976.

656. UNESCO. 'Women and Education in the World Today' (ED/WS/183). Paris, 1970.

657. Ungor, Berait Zeki. 'Women in the Middle East and North Africa and Universal Suffrage.' *Annals of the American Academy of Political and Social Sciences* (Jan. 1968):72–81.

658. UNICEF. Executive Board, 1972 Session. 'General Progress Report of the Executive Director. Programme Developments in the Eastern Mediterranean. Summary of the Report on Women and Girls in National Development' (E/ICEF/616/Add. 3/Annex), Feb. 1972.

659. UNICEF. 'Role of Arab Women in National Development.' Paper presented at the Seminar on Arab Women in National Development, Cairo, Egypt, 24–30 Sept., 1972.

660. UNICEF. 'Seminar on the Role of Women in Integrated Rural Development with Emphasis on Population Problems.' Cairo, Egypt, 26 Oct.–3 Nov., 1974.

662. UNICEF. *Womanpower in the Third World.* (A Packet of Materials for a Unit on Women in Developing Countries.) Brooklyn: Brooklyn College, 1972.

663. UNICEF. *Women and Development.* (Prepared in Consultation with ILO, FAO, UNESCO and WHO). New York: United Nations, Sept. 1975.

664. United Nations. Economic and Social Council. Commission on the Status of Women. 'Participation of Women in the Economic and Social Development of their Countries' (E/CN. 6/513). New York, 1970.

665. United Nations. Economic and Social Council. Commission on the Status of Women. 'Programme of Concerted International Action to Promote the Advancement of Women and their Integration in Development. Implementation of a Programme of

Concerted International Action.' Report of the Secretary General, n.d.

666. United Nations. Economic and Social Council. Commission on the Status of Women. 'Report on the Status of Arab Women' (E/CN. 6/597), 1976.

667. United Nations. Economic and Social Council. Commission on the Status of Women, 25th Session. 'Study on the Equality of Access of Girls and Women to Education in the Context of Rural Development.' Report prepared by UNESCO, n.d.

668. United Nations. Economic and Social Council. Commission on the Status of Women. *Study on the Interrelationship of the Status of Women and Family Planning* (E/CN. 6/575/Add. 1), Dec. 1973.

669. United Nations. Economic and Social Council. Commission on the Status of Women, 25th Session. 'Study on the Interrelationship of the Status of Women and Family Planning.' Report of the Special Rapporteur Addendum (2).

670. United Nations. Economic and Social Council. 'Housing for the Single Worker in Developing Areas. Statement submitted by the International Federation of Business and Professional Women, a non-governmental organization in consultative status, Category 1, July 5, 1978' (E/1978/NGO/4).

671. United Nations. Economic Commission for Western Asia. 'Expert Group Meeting on the Integration of Women in Development' (E/ECWA/NR/CIT. 1/ INF. 2/Rev. 1). Amman, Jordan, 15–20 Apr., 1978.

672. United Nations. Economic Commission for Western Asia. 'Plan of Action for the Integration of Women in Development adopted for the Region of the Economic and Social Commission for Asia and the Pacific' (E/ECWA/SDHS/CONF. 2/6), 1978.

673. United Nations. Economic Commission for Western Asia. 'A Preliminary Report on the Status and Participation of Women in Development in Selected Countries of the ECWA Region' (ECWA/HR/L.2 Corr. 1), 1974.

674. United Nations. Economic Commission for Western

Asia. 'Regional Conference for the Integration of Women in Development' (E/ECWA/NR/CTT.1/ INF.2/Rev.1). Amman, Jordan, 29 May–4 June, 1978.

675. United Nations. Economic Commission for Western Asia. 'Regional Plan of Action for the Integration of Women in Development for the ECWA Region' (E/ECWA/SDHS/CONF. 2/8).

676. United Nations. Economic Commission for Western Asia. 'Regional Plan of Action for the Integration of Women in Development for the Countries of the ECWA Region' (E/ECWA/69 Add. 1), 1978.

677. United Nations. International Labor Organization. Office for Women Workers' Questions. *Women at Work*, 1977– , 3 times a year. (News bulletin published by the Office for Women Workers' Questions.)

678. United Nations. International Labor Organization. *Women Workers and Society. International Perspectives*. Geneva: ILO, 1976.

679. United Nations. Office of Public Information. *Meeting in Mexico, World Conference of the International Women's Year, 1975*.

680. United Nations. Office of Public Information. *Equal Rights for Women. International Women's Year*, 1975.

682. Vacca, V. 'Le associazioni femminili chiedono il voto per le donne.' (Women's Associations Claim the Right of Voting for Women.) *Oriente Moderno* 40, 1 (1960): 13.

683. Vacca, V. 'Il V congresso dell'unione femminile araba a Beirut.' (Fifth Congress of the Arab Women's Union in Beirut.) *Oriente Moderno* 14, 6 (1934): 280–281.

684. Vajrathon, Mallica and Singh, Jyoti. 'Women, Population and Development.' *World Education* no. 14 (April 1977).

685. Vajrathon, Mallica and Singh, Jyoti. *Women and the New East*. Washington, D.C.: Middle East Institute, 1960.

686. Van Dusen, Roxann A. 'Integrating Women into National Economies: Programming Considerations with Special Reference to the Near East.' Submitted to Office of Technical Support, Near East Bureau, Agency for International Development, Washington, D.C., July 1977.

687. Van Dusen, Roxann A. 'The Study of Women in the Middle East: some Thoughts.' *Middle East Studies Association Bulletin* 10, 2 (May 1976):1–20.

688. Vernier, Pierre. 'Education for Arab Girls—Economic Expansion and Changing Attitudes Favor Progress.' *UNESCO Features* 437 (Apr. 1964):14–17.

689. Vernier, Pierre. 'La scolarisation des jeunes filles arabes, le départ est donné.' *Informations, UNESCO* (30 Apr., 1964):14–17.

690. Viguera Franco, E. de. 'La condicion de la mujer en el derecho arabe et islamico.' *Cuadernos de Estudios Africanos* 4 (1948):77–91.

691. Wahaib, Abdul Amir. 'Education and Status of Women in the Middle East with Special Reference to Egypt, Tunisia and Iraq.' Ph.D. dissertation, Southern Illinois University, 1970.

692. Wajihuddin, Ahmed. 'Women: the First Domestic Animal.' *People* 2, 2 (1975):24.

693. Wakim, Edward. 'Veiled Revolution.' *Midstream* 81 (Autumn 1959).

694. Wali, Abdel Gabber. 'Research and Communication.' Paper presented at the Seminar on the Role of Women in Integrated Rural Development with Emphasis on Population Problems, Cairo, Egypt, 26 Oct.–3 Nov., 1974.

695. Ward, Barbara E. 'Women and Technology in Developing Countries.' *Impact of Science on Society* 20, 1 (1970):93–101.

696. Watson, Hanan. 'The Role of Women in a Developing Society.' *Arab World* 13, 2 (Feb. 1967):3–6.

697. Weisblat, A.M. *The Role of Rural Women in Development: a Seminar Report*. New York: Agricultural Development Council, Research and Training Network, Oct. 1975.

698. Westphal-Hellbusch, Sigrid. 'Transvestiten bei arabischen Stämmen.' *Sociologus* 6, 2 (1956):126–137.
699. Wingate, R.O. 'Moslem Women in Palestine and Syria.' *World Dominion* (1934):177–185.
700. 'Without my Veil I was Suddenly Free.' *Dagens Nyheter*, 3 Aug., 1973. (Swedish Newspaper.)
701. 'Women and Modern Secular Education in the Arab East.' Paper presented at the 10th Annual Meeting of the Middle East Studies Association, Los Angeles 10–13 Nov., 1976.
702. *Women in the Middle East*. Cambridge, Mass.: Women's Middle East Collective, 1973. (Anthology of Articles, from P.O. Box 134, West Newton, Mass. 02156.)
703. 'Women in Rural Development and Index, Nos. 1–6, Part II, 1974–1977.' *Rural Development Network Bulletin* no. 6, Part II (May 1977).
704. 'Women's Role in the Development of Tropical and Sub-Tropical Countries.' *Report of the 31st Meeting of the International Institute of Differing Civilizations*, Brussels, 1958.
705. 'Women's Year in the Middle East.' Centre d'Etudes pour le Monde Arabe Moderne Reports, *Islamic Law and Change in Arab Society*. Beirut: Dar el-Mashreq, 1976, pp. 123–169.
706. Wood, Lucie A. 'An Inquiry into the Preference for Parallel Cousin Marriage Among the Contemporary Arabs.' Ph.D. dissertation, Columbia University, New York, 1959.
707. Woodsmall, Ruth F. *Study of the Role of Women, their Activities and Organizations in Lebanon, Egypt, Iraq, Jordan and Syria, Oct. 1954–Aug. 1955*. Sponsored by the International Federation of Business and Professional Women. Woodstock, Vt.: Elm Tree Press, 1956.
708. 'Working Paper: Review of Conditions Affecting the Integration of Rural Women in Ten Countries of FAO's Asia and the Far East and Near East Regions' (ESH:IRWD/77/1), 1977.
709. Yammine, Randa. 'It's a Woman's World.' *Monday Morning*, 14–20 July, 1975, pp. 33–61.

710. Yasseen, Shahzanan. *Collaboration between International Organizations and Arab Middle East States to Improve the Status of Women.* Institut de Hautes Etudes Internationales, June 1972.

711. Youssef, Nadia. 'Cultural Ideals, Feminine Behaviour and Family Control.' *Comparative Studies in Society and History* 15, 3 (1973): 326–347.

712. Youssef, Nadia. 'Differential Labor Force Participation of Women in Latin American and Middle Eastern Countries: the Influence of Family Characteristics.' *Social Forces* 51, 2 (Dec. 1972): 135–153.

713. Youssef, Nadia. 'Social Structure and the Female Labor Force: the Case of Women Workers in Muslim Middle Eastern Countries.' *Demography* 8, 4 (Nov. 1971): 427–439.

714. Youssef, Nadia. 'Social Structure and Female Labor Force Participation in Developing Countries: a Comparison of Latin American and Middle Eastern Countries.' Ph.D. dissertation, University of California, Berkeley, 1970.

715. Youssef, Nadia. 'Women's Status and Fertility in Muslim Countries of the Middle East and Asia.' Paper presented at the American Psychological Association Annual Meeting, New Orleans, La., 1974.

716. Youssef, Nadia. *Women and Work in Developing Societies.* Population Monograph Series, no. 15. Berkeley: University of California, Institute of International Studies, 1974.

717. Zanati, Mahmoud S. *The Relation Between Men and Women Among the Arabs.* Cairo: Dar el Gameat el Masria, 1959.

718. El Zayyat, L. 'Une femme engagée.' *Eléments* no. 8–9 (1971): 43–46.

719. Zurayk, Huda. 'The Changing Role of Arab Women.' Paper presented at the Seminar on Population Development in the ECWA Region. Amman, Jordan, 18–30 Nov., 1978.

Women in North Africa— General Works

720. Accad, Evelyne. 'La longue marche des héroines des romans modernes du Machrek et du Maghreb.' *Présence Francophone* no. 12 (Spring 1976):3–11.
721. Accad, Evelyne. 'Themes of Sexual repression in the North African Novelists.' Paper presented at the African Studies Conference, Calif., 1975.
722. Adnane, L. 'Trois africaines à Paris, marocaine, algérienne, tunisienne.' *Jeune Afrique* no. 301 (16 Oct., 1966).
723. Anastase Marie de St. Elie. 'La femme du désert autrefois et aujourd'hui.' *Anthropos* 3 (1908):53–67, 181–192.
724. El-Annabi, Tayyib. 'Le divorce dans la loi et la société.' *Revue de l'Institut des Belles Lettres Arabes* (1967): 274–278.
725. Asfar, Gabriel V. 'Women and Legend in Sauf.' Paper presented at the 7th Annual Middle East Studies Association Meeting, Milwaukee, Wis., 8–10 Nov., 1973.
726. Bentami, Rosalie. *L'enfer de la casbah*. Paris: Hachette, n.d.; Alger: Imprimerie du Lycee, n.d.
727. 'Bibliography on Female Genital Mutilation.' *WIN News* 4, 4 (Autumn 1978):44.
728. Borrmans, Maurice. 'Contributions à l'étude des mentalités sur la famille: ce qu'en pensent de jeunes sahariens.' *Revue de l'Occident Musulman et de la Méditerranée* no. 5 (1er et 2ème semestre 1968): 15–39.

729. Boubaker, H. 'La musulmane nord-africaine d'aujourd' hui.' *Rythmes du Monde* 5, 4 (1950):25–33. (Also in *Synthèse* (Dec. 1951):26–33 and *Ecrits de Paris* (Dec. 1953):48–55.)

730. Callens, M. 'La femme kabyle.' *En Terre d'Islam* (Jan. 1929):12–25.

732. Daguin, A. *Le mariage dans les pays musulmans, particulièrement en Tunisie, en Algérie et dans le Soudan.* Paris: Lucien Dorban, n.d.

733. Denison, S.M. 'A Moorish Woman's Life.' *Muslim World* 11 (1921):24–28.

734. Desanti, Dominique. 'Une enquête sur la femme africaine.' *Jeune Afrique* 188–189 (1964):29–31.

735. Desportes, E. 'Théorie de la dot en droit musulman et dans les coutumes berbères.' *Revue Algérienne* Part I (1949):13–38.

736. Despres, L. 'Evolution de la musulmane en Afrique du Nord.' *En Terre d'Islam* (May 1928):103–110; (June 1928):140–144; (July 1928):190–195.

737. Devulder, M. 'Rituel magique des femmes kabyles.' *Revue Africaine* Part 3–4 (1957):299–362.

738. 'Le divorce.' *Révolution Africaine*, 1964, pp. 6–8.

739. Doumergue, G. 'La femme kabyle, quelques remarques sur le décret du 19 Mai 1931.' *Revue des Etudes Islamiques* 5 (1931):1–19.

740. Duvignaud, Jean. *Change at Shebika: Report from a North African Village.* Translated by Frances Frenaye. New York: Random House—Vintage Books, 1970.

741. 'Une enquête de révolution africaine sur le divorce.' *Revue de Presse* no. 91 (Jan. 1965).

742. Etienne, B. 'Colloque sur la participation de la femme rurale au développement économique et social.' *Annuaire de l'Afrique du Nord* (CNRS), (1968): 831–834.

743. Evans-Pritchard, Edward E. *Kinship and Marriage Among the Nuer.* Oxford: Clarendon Press, 1951.

744. 'L'évolution du statut personnel en Afrique nord depuis l'indépendance.' *Maghreb* 43 (Jan.–Feb. 1971): 29–43.

745. 'Female Circumcision: Summary Facts/Africa and Bibliography.' *Women's International Network News* 2, 2 (Spring 1976): 16–24; 2, 3 (Summer 1976): 19–24.

746. Fernande, Lucas. 'La femme musulmane: enquête dans le nord-africain.' *En Terre d'Islam* no. 47 (1931): 186–193.

747. Fontaine, C. 'De la femme objet à la femme sujet: évolution de la femme en Afrique "du Nord".' *Revue de Psychologie des Peuples* 18, 3 (3 Trim. 1963): 273–282.

748. Francos, Anya. 'Une militante.' *Jeune Afrique* no. 671 (17 Nov., 1973): 62–63.

749. Hafkin, Nancy J. and Bay, E.J., eds. *Women in Africa*. Stanford: Stanford University Press, 1976.

750. el-Hamamsy, Laila Shukry. *The Role of Women in the Development of Tropical and Sub-Tropical Countries*. Brussels: International Institute of Differing Civilizations, 1958.

751. el-Hamamsy, Laila Shukry. 'The Political Role of Women in Tropical and Sub-Tropical Countries.' Cairo, 1960.

752. Hosken, Franziska P. *The Hosken Report, Genital and Sexual Mutilation of Females*. Mass.: Women's International Network News, 1979.

753. Huston, Perdita. 'Being a Woman.' (Sudan, Egypt, Tunisia.) *World Education* no. 14 (Apr. 1977).

754. Huston, Perdita. *Message from the Village*. New York: Epoch B. Foundation, 1978.

755. Joubin, Odette. 'L'incidence de la scolarisation sur l'intégration des femmes musulmanes à une société moderne, deux exemples: la Tunisie et le Maroc.' Thèse, Université de Paris, 1966.

756. Lucas, F. 'La femme musulmane: enquête dans le nord-africain.' *En Terre d'Islam* no. 47 (1931): 186–193.

757. 'Maternity Protection in Selected African Countries: a Table.' *Women at Work* (ILO) no. 3 (1977): 14–18.

758. Mikhail, Mona. 'The Image of Women in North African Literature: Myth or Reality.' Paper presented at

the 7th Annual Middle East Studies Association Meeting, Milwaukee, Wis., 8–10 Nov., 1973. (Also in *American Journal of Arabic Studies* 3 (1975): 37–47). Washington D.C.: Three Continents Press, 1978.

759. Mokarzel, S.A. 'Le monde des femmes et son entrée dans la cité.' *Information Rapide* (Alger), nos. 8–10 (Dec. 1967):1–48.

760. 'The Mutilation of Female Genitalia (Female Circumcision, Clitoridectomy and Infibulation.' *WIN News* 2 (Jan. 1976):30–44.

761. Paolini, John. 'The Kabyle Handling of Grief.' *Muslim World* 59, 3–4 (July–Oct. 1969):251–274.

762. Paulme, Denise. *La mère dévorante: essai sur la morphologie des contes africains.* Paris: Gallimard, 1976.

763. Pieters, Guy and Lowenfels, A.B. 'Infibulation in the Horn of Africa.' *New York State Journal of Medicine* 77 (Apr. 1977): 729–731.

764. 'A propos du mariage mixte.' *Dialogue* 44 (7 July, 1975):32–33; 45 (15 July, 1975):36–37; 47 (28 July, 1975):22–23; 48 (Aug. 1975):24–27; 49 (4 Aug., 1975):18–20.

765. Roberds, Frances E. 'Moslem Women of North Africa.' *Muslim World* 27 (1937):362–369.

766. Roques, Prete. 'Education et formation professionnelle féminine dans les états africains d'expression française.' *Afrique Contemporaine* (Nov.–Dec. 1965): 18–26.

767. Skarzynska, K. 'Moeurs et rites nuptiaux chez quelques groupes ethniques d'Egypte, de Nubie et de Libye, d'après les récents travaux arabes.' *Folia Orientalia* (Cracow) 4 (1962):343–352.

768. Stiehm, Judith H. 'Measuring Women's Power.' Paper presented at the Wellesley Conference on Women and Development, Wellesley College, Mass., 2–6 June, 1976.

769. Tillion, G. *Le harem et les cousins.* Paris: Editions du Seuil, 1966. (Résumé available in *Revue de l'Institut des Belles Lettres Arabes* 30 (1967):309–316.)

770. United Nations. Economic Commission for Africa.

ECA Five-Year Programme on Pre-Vocational and Vocational Training of Girls and Women Toward Their Full Participation in Development, 1972–1976.

771. United Nations. Economic Commission for Africa and the German Foundation for Developing Countries. *Regional Conference on Education, Vocational Training and Work Opportunities for Girls and Women in African Countries.*

772. United Nations. Economic Commission for Africa. Human Resources Development Division. Women's Programme Unit. *The Changing and Contemporary Role of Women in African Development*, Jan. 1974.

773. United Nations. Economic Commission for Africa. Human Resources Development Division. Women's Programme Unit. 'Women and National Development in African Countries: some Profound Contradictions.' Paper presented at the Ford Foundation Task Force on Women, Addis Ababa, Ethiopia, Feb., 1973.

774. United Nations. Economic Commission for Western Asia. 'Plan of Action for the Integration of Women in Development Adopted for the Region of the Economic Commission for Africa' (E/ECWA/SDHS/CONF.2/5), 1978.

775. United Nations. World Health Organization. 'Traditional Practices Affecting the Health of Women and Children.' Khartoum, Sudan, 10–15 Feb., 1979.

776. Vinogradov, Amal Rassam. 'Man's World, Women's Place: The Politics of Sex in North Africa.' Ann Arbor, Mich., 1973.

777. Vinogradov, Amal Rassam. (Amal Rassam.) 'What Price Women? The Evolution of the Status of Women Among the Ait Ndhir of the Middle Atlas.' Paper presented at the 7th Annual Middle East Studies Association Meeting, Milwaukee, Wis., 8–10 Nov., 1973.

778. Watson, A. Dorothy. 'Women of the Western Sahara Desert.' *Muslim World* 39 (Apr. 1949):97–101.

779. 'WIN News List of Female Genital Mutilation in

Africa: Countries/Regions/Populations.' *WIN News* 3 (Autumn 1977):49.

780. 'Women and Health: Circumcision and Infibulation of Females.' *WIN News* 1, 3 (June 1975):39–41; 1, 4 (Oct. 1975):35–41; 2, 4 (Autumn 1976):29–34; 3, 2 (Spring 1977):29–41.

781. 'Women and Health: Female Circumcision.' *WIN News* 2, 1 (Jan. 1976):30–44; 3, 3 (Summer 1977):24–29; 3, 1 (Winter 1977):25–29.

Women in Individual Arab Countries

ALGERIA

782. Abu-Abdallah. 'L'adolescente algérienne.' *Révolution Africaine*, 12 Dec., 1964.
783. Accad, Evelyne. 'Feminist Revolution in the Algerian Revolution: a Dead End? Reflection of Feminist Consciousness in Asia Djebar.' Paper presented at the Modern Language Association Conference, Calif., 1975.
784. 'Algerie: algériennes en lutte pour les droits élémentaires des femmes algériennes.' *WIN News* 4, 4 (Autumn 1978):63. (Groupes Femmes Algériennes, Librairie Floreal, 121 Avenue du Maine, 75014, Paris, France.)
785. 'L'algérienne au travail.' *Révolution Africaine*, 1964, pp. 6–8.
786. Aouissi, Cheikh Mechri. 'Les causes classiques de l'instabilité du mariage.' *Revue Algérienne des Sciences Juridiques, Economiques et Politiques* 5, 4 (1968):1091–1099.
787. Arnaud, Gabriel. 'Une algérienne se revolte.' *Terre Entière* 7 (Jan./Feb. 1970):76–99.
788. Barrire, G. 'La veuvage à Idelés (Ahaggar).' *Travaux de l'Institut de Recherches Sahariennes* 24 (1965): 177–182.
789. Beauvoir, Simone de and Halimi, Gisele. *Djamila

Boupacha. Translated by Peter Green. London: André Deutsch & Weidenfeld and Nicolson, 1962.

790. Benatia, Farouk. 'L'algérienne et le travail salarié.' *Algérie-Actualité* no. 215, 1969, pp. 4–5.

791. Benatia, Farouk. 'L'enseignement au féminin: l'enseignement authentique de la femme.' *Algérie-Actualité* no. 210, 1969, pp. 10–11.

792. Benatia, Farouk. *Le travail féminin en Algérie*. Alger: Société Nationale d'Edition et de Diffusion, 1970.

793. Benatia, M. 'Le travail dans le département d'Alger.' Thèse de 3ème Cycle, Université de Bordeaux, 1969.

794. Bitat, Zohra and Belmihoud, M. 'Existe-t-il un problème de la femme algérienne?' *Confluent* 32–33 (1963):493–499.

795. Blanc, A. 'L'évolution intellectuelle, morale et sociale de la jeune fille musulmane en Algérie.' *Revue de Psychologie des Peuples* 13 (1958):306–323.

796. Boals, Kathryn. 'Women and Revolutionary Politics.' Paper presented at the 7th Annual Middle East Studies Association Meeting, Milwaukee, Wis., 8–10 Nov., 1973.

797. Boals, Kay and Stiehm, J. 'The Politics of Ambivalence: Male–Female Relations in Algeria.' Paper presented at the Symposium on Social and Political Change: the Role of Women, jointly sponsored by the University of California, Santa Barbara and the Center for the Study of Democratic Institutions, 1974.

798. Boals, Kay and Stiehm, J. 'The Women of Liberated Algeria.' *Center for the Study of Democratic Institutions Magazine* 7, 3 (1974):75.

799. Boissenot. 'L'évolution de la femme algérienne.' Mémoire. Paris, Centre des Hautes Etudes Administratives sur l'Afrique et l'Asie Moderne (CHEAM), no. 3232, 1960.

800. Borrmans, M. 'Perspectives algériennes en matière de droit familial.' *Studia Islamica* 37 (1973):129–153.

801. Boubaker, F. *et al.* 'Les femmes des hautes plaines

constantinoises vues par elles-mêmes.' *Revue Algér-ienne des Sciences Juridiques, Economiques et Politiques* II, 3 (1974):161–164.

802. Bousquet-Lefèvre, Laure. *La femme kabyle.* Paris: Librairie du Recueil Sirey, 1939.

803. Bousquet, G.H. 'Les mariages mixtes à l'état civil d'Alger.' *Révolution Africaine,* 1950–1960, pp. 190–193.

804. Bousquet, G.H. 'Remarques sur quelques bida obser-vées chez les musulmans d'Algérie.' *Die Welt des Islams* no. 1 (1954):34–45.

805. Boutémène, Yahia. 'La condition de la femme musul-mane en Algérie.' Paris, Centre des Hautes Etudes Administratives sur l'Afrique et l'Asie Moderne (CHEAM), no. 3406, 1960.

806. Chamla, Marie-Claude and Demoulin, F. *Croissance des Algériens de l'enfance à l'age adulte.* Paris: Editions du Centre National de la Recherche Scientifique, 1976.

807. Charroin, J. 'Femmes kabyles dans la famille patriar-cale.' *Etudes Sociales Nord-Africaines* I, Cahiers 7–8 (Aug.–Sept. 1950).

808. Corrèze, Françoise. *Femme des Mechtas: témoignage sur l'Est algérien.* Paris: Les Editeurs Français Réunis, 1976.

809. 'Débat public sur les mariages mixtes en Algérie.' *Hommes et Migrations: Documents* 19, 734 (1968): 6.

810. Debèche, Djamila. *Aziza.* Algér: Imprimerie Imbert, 1935.

811. Debèche, Djamila. *Leila, jeune fille algérienne.* Alger: Imprimerie Charras, 1947.

812. Debèche, Djamila. 'Les lettres et la femme algérienne.' Conférence donnée à la Société des Arts et des Lettres à l'Hôtel de ville d'Alger, 16 Jan., 1951.

813. Dejeux, J. 'Connaissance du monde féminin et de la famille en Algérie (essai de synthèse documentaire), 1947–1967.' *Revue Algérienne des Sciences Juridi-ques, Economiques et Politiques* 5, 4 (1968):1247–1311.

814. Dejeux, J. 'Romans sur les milieux féminins algériens.' *Cahiers Nord-Africains* 82 (Feb.–Mar. 1961):53–61.

815. Dionisi, Bianca. 'A proposito del III congresso dell'-Union Nationale des Femmes Algériennes.' *Oriente Moderno* 55, 1–2 (Jan.–Feb. 1975):62–66.

816. 'Le donne algerine.' *Rassegna del Mondo Arabo* no. 1 (1969):25–40.

817. 'Dossiers sur le problème de la femme algérienne.' *Information Rapide* 2, 4 (Nov. 1963):3–34.

818. Douedar, Marysa. 'Libération du mariage.' *Revue Algérienne des Sciences Juridiques, Economiques et Politiques* 11, 3 (1974):133–147.

819. Estivals, G. 'Algerian Women.' *Holiday* 37 (June 1965): 60–61.

820. Etienne, Bruno. *Algérie, culture et révolution.* Paris: Editions du Seuil, 1977.

821. 'L'évolution de la femme algérienne.' *Revue de Presse* no. 75 (May 1963).

822. Faivre, Charles. *Les étrangers d'auvergne—les migrants en Suisse. La femme algérienne.* Paris: Etudes Sociales Nord-Africaines (E.S.N.A.), 1969.

823. Farrag, Amina. 'Social Control Amongst the Mzabite Women of Beni-Isguen.' *Middle Eastern Studies* 7, 3 (1971):317–28.

824. Fauque, L.P. 'La femme dans la société algérienne.' *L'Afrique et l'Asie* 76 (1966):2–14.

825. Fauque, L.P. 'Le mariage des musulmans algériens.' *Revue Algérienne, Tunisienne et Marocaine de Législation et Jurisprudence* 77, 4 (July–Aug. 1961): 59–68.

826. Fauque, L.P. 'L'oeuvre française émancipatrice de la femme musulmane d'Algérie.' *Bulletin de Liaison et de Documentation des Affaires Algériennes* (Jan./Feb. 1962):16–17.

827. 'La femme et la jeunesse dans l'Algérie d'aujourd'hui.' *France Algérie* no. 17 (April–May 1967):8–11.

828. 'La femme et la vie politique en Algérie.' *Maghreb* (Paris) no. 39 (May–June 1970):32–41.

829. 'La femme et l'édification de l'Algérie socialiste.' *Revue de Presse* Part 76 (1963).

830. 'La femme dans la société algérienne.' *L'Afrique et l'Asie* no. 76 (1966): 2–14.

831. Foudil, Abdel Kader. 'De quelques causes modernes d'instabilité du mariage, de la procédure en matière de divorce et du rôle du juge.' *Revue Algérienne des Sciences Juridiques, Economiques et Politiques* 5, 4, (1968): 1101–1105.

832. François, S.M. 'La politesse féminine kabyle, aspects religieux, aspects superstitieux, les cadeaux, l'hospitalité.' *Revue de l'Institut des Belles Lettres Arabes* (1951): 35–56.

833. 'Freedom of Choice in Algerian Marriage.' *Muslim World* 55 (1965): 279–281.

834. Gaudry, Mathéa. *La femme chaouia de l'Aurès: étude de sociologie berbère.* Paris: Paul Geuthner, 1929.

835. Gaudry, Mathéa. *La société féminine au Djébel Amour et au Ksel: étude de sociologie rurale nord-africaine.* Paris: Paul Geuthner, 1961.

836. Gaudry, Mathéa. 'L'instruction de la femme indigène en Algérie.' *Afrique Française* (Dec. 1935 and Jan. 1936).

837. Goichon, Amélie Marie. *La vie féminine du Mzab: étude de sociologie musulmane.* Paris: Paul Geuthner 1927.

838. Gordon, David C. *Women of Algeria: An Essay on Change.* Cambridge, Mass.: Harvard University Press, 1968.

839. Haroun, Mohammed Ali. 'Les causes modernes d'instabilité du mariage.' *Revue Algérienne* (1968): 1127–1138.

840. Heggoy, Alf Andrew. 'Algerian Women and the Right to Vote: Some Colonial Anomalies.' *Muslim World* 64, 3 (1974): 228–235.

841. Heggoy, Alf Andrew. 'Cultural Disrespect: European and Algerian Views on Women in Colonial and Independent Algeria.' *Muslim World* 62, 2 (1972): 323–334.

842. Heggoy, Alf Andrew. 'On the Evolution of Algerian Women.' *African Studies Review* 17 (1974): 449–456.

843. Hennebelle, G. 'La situation de la femme en Algérie-

théâtre.' *L'Afrique Littéraire et Artistique* no. 13 (Oct. 1970):49–57.

844. Honoré-Laine, Geneviève. 'A l'heure de la révolution algérienne—attitudes féminines dans "la Femme dans la Vie Sociale" (Union Féminine Civique et Sociale, 37 rue de Valois, Paris).' *Documents Nord-Africains* no. 540 (4 Nov. 1963):1–5.

845. Howe, Sonia E. 'Touareg Women and their Veiled Men.' *Muslim World* 18, 1 (1928):34–44.

846. ILO. Technical Cooperation Report. *Algérie: Institut national de formation professionnelle des adultes—memorandum technique sur la formation professionnelle féminine en Algérie* (UNDP/SF 68–2–c–2–1). Genève, 1969.

847. Issad, Mohand. 'Le role du juge et la volonté des parties dans le rupture du lien conjugal.' *Revue Algérienne* (1968):1065–1090.

848. 'Les jeunes algériens et le problème de la mixité.' *Documents Nord-Africains* no. 589 (1964):1–12.

849. 'Jeunes travailleuses algériennes.' *Hommes et Migrations: Documents* no. 640 (1966):1–8.

850. 'Jeunesse féminine algérienne.' *Revue de Presse* no. 92 (Feb. 1965).

851. Keenan, Jeremy. 'Power and Wealth are Cousins: Descent, Class and Marital Strategies among the Kel Ahaggar (Tuareg-Sahara).' *Africa: Journal of the International African Institute* 47 (1977):333–343.

852. Keenan, Jeremy. 'The Tuareg Veil.' *Middle East Studies* 13, 1 (Jan. 1977):3–13.

853. 'Kif-Kif la française.' *Time*, 23 Feb., 1959, p. 26.

854. Kirkpatrick, Jean S. 'Being a Mayor in Algeria is no Easy Job for a Woman.' *New York Times*, 10 July, 1975.

855. Koura, Salah-Eddine. 'Le divorce et la répudiation en droit musulman (Charia) et le droit positif algérien.' *Revue Algérienne des Sciences Juridiques, Economiques et Politiques* 11, 3 (1974):111–112.

856. Laine, Geneviève. 'La femme et l'enfant dans l'Algérie nouvelle.' *La Croix*, 29 May, 1963.

857. Lefèbvre, G. 'Le portage de l'eau dans deux villages de Petite Kabylie.' *Libyca* 9–10 (1961–1962):199–204.

858. Lefèbvre, G. 'La toilette féminine dans deux villages de Petite Kabylie.' *Libyca* 11 (1963):199–220.

859. Lewis, F. 'No Revolution for the Women of Algiers.' *New York Times Magazine*, 29 Oct., 1967, 28.

860. Marchand, Henri. *La musulmane algérienne*. Rodez: Editions Subervie, 1960.

861. Marchand, Henri. 'La musulmane algérienne et la réconciliation franco-musulmane.' *Comptes Rendus Mensuels des Séances de l'Académie des Sciences d'Outre-Mer* (1959):269–282.

862. Marchant, A. 'A la rencontre des jeunes algériennes.' *Croissance des Jeunes Nations* no. 86 (Mar. 1969): 21–28.

863. 'Le mariage de jeunes algériennes.' *Revue de Presse* 74 (1963).

864. Marmey, P. 'Le droit de vote de la femme musulmane algérienne.' Unpublished mémoire. Paris, Centre des Hautes Etudes Administratives sur l'Afrique et l'Asie Moderne (CHEAM), no. 2909, 1958.

865. Miner, Horace M. and DeVos George. *Oasis and Casbah: Algerian Culture and Personality in Change*. Ann Arbor: University of Michigan, 1960.

866. M'rabet, Fadéla. *Les algériennes*. Paris: Maspero, 1967.

867. M'rabet, Fadéla. *La femme algérienne suivi de les algériennes*. Paris: Maspero, 1969.

868. Narbeth, E.G. 'Evangelism among Women and Girls in Urban Algeria.' *Muslim World* 37, 4 (1947): 266–277.

869. 'No Easy Exit from Slavery behind the Veil.' *People* 2, 1 (1973):3–6.

870. Portier, L. 'Débat public sur les mariages mixtes en Algérie.' *Terre Entière* 24 (July–Aug. 1967):67–81.

871. Roche, M.H. 'The Moslem Women of Algeria.' *Muslim World* 23 (1933):290–295.

872. 'Le rôle de la femme dans l'Algérie nouvelle.' *Revue de Presse* no. 65 (May–June 1962).

873. Roussier, Jules. 'Déclaration à l'état civil et preuve de mariage conclu "more islamico" en Algérie. La loi de 11–7–57 no. 57777.' *Revue Algérienne, Tunisienne, et Marocaine de Législation et Jurisprudence* 74 (1958):1–11.

874. Roussier, Jules. 'Mariage et divorce des musulmans algériens.' *Le Développement Africain* 2, 3–4: 7–10.

875. Roussier, Jules. 'Mariage et divorce en Algérie.' *Die Welt des Islams* VI, 3–4 (1961):248–254.

876. Roussier, Jules. *Le mariage et sa dissolution dans le statut civil local algérien*. Algiers, 1960.

877. Schoen, C. 'Note sur le mariage et le divorce des musulmans d'origine algérienne.' *Hommes et Migrations* 17, 665 (1966):1–10.

878. 'La scolarisation des jeunes filles musulmanes en Algérie.' *Documents Nord-Africans* no. 410 (1960).

879. 'La situation de la femme en Algérie: tragédie ou comédie.' *Jeune Afrique* no. 507 (1970):38–40.

880. 'La socialisation des jeunes filles en Algérie.' *Djeich* no. 64 (Sept. 1968):17–19.

881. Stiehm, Judith *et al.* 'Judicial Tests of the Congruency of Law and Culture: Women's Status in Algeria, France and the U.S.' Paper presented at the International Political Science Association Congress, Edinburgh, Aug. 16–21, 1976.

882. Tabutin, Dominique. 'La polygamie en Algérie.' *Population* 24, 2 (Mar.–Apr. 1974):313–326.

883. Touat, L. *Le monde des femmes et son entrée dans la cité*. Alger: Sécrétariat Social d'Alger, 1967.

884. Vallin, Jacques. *Age moyen au premier mariage des hommes et des femmes en Algérie*. Oran: C.N.R.P., 1973.

885. Vallin, Jacques. 'Facteurs économiques de l'âge au mariage de la femme algérienne.' *Algérie du Nord* (1973):1172–1176.

886. Vallin, Jacques. *Variations géographiques de l'âge moyen au premier mariage des femmes algériennes*. Oran: C.N.R.P., 1973.

887. Vasse, Denis. 'La femme algérienne.' *Travaux et Jours* 13 (Apr.–June 1964):85–102.
888. Vigier, René. *La succession 'ab intestat' de la femme kabyle en Grande Kabylie*. Paris: Editions Vega, 1932.
889. Villot, Etienne Cecile E. *Moeurs, coutumes et institutions des indigènes de l'Algérie*. Alger: Librairie Adolphe Jourdan, 1888.
890. Wakefield, Frances M. 'Twareg Women of the Sahara.' *Muslim World* 39 (Jan. 1949):6.
891. 'Women and Work in Constitutions: Algeria.' *Women at Work* (ILO) 2 (1977):7–8.
892. 'Women in Algeria.' *WIN News* 5, 1 (Winter 1979):50.
893. Young, Ian. *The Private Life of Islam*. London: Allen Lane, 1974.
894. Zerdoumi, N. 'L'emancipation de la femme, extrait d'un mémoire de l'auteur.' *Revue de Presse* no. 81 (Jan. 1964).
895. Zerdoumi, N. 'La fille de la campagne en Algérie.' *Carnets de l'Enfance* 7 (Jan. 1973):128–137.

BAHRAIN

896. 'Bahreïn.' *WIN News* 2 (Spring 1976):45.
897. Dowaicher, Safia Muhammad. 'Development of Women's Education in Bahrain.' M.A. thesis, American University of Beirut, Beirut, 1964.
898. 'The Emancipation of Women in Bahrain Started Later than in Other Arab Countries.' *Le Monde*, 3 Feb., 1976. (Also in *WIN News* 2, 2 (Spring 1976):45.)
899. Greene, Marilyn. 'Girls Streak Ahead.' *Gulf Mirror*, 20–26 Nov., 1977, p. 19.
900. Hansen, Henry Harold. *Investigation in a Shi'a Village in Bahrain*. Copenhagen: Publications of the National Museum, 1967.

D

901. Hansen, Henry Harold. 'The Patterns of Women's Seclusion and Veiling in a Shia Village (Bahrain).' *Folk* 3 (1961):23–42.
902. Taki, Ali Hassan. *The Changing Status of the Bahrain Women.* Bahrain: Oriental Press, n.d.
903. Taki, Ali Hassan. 'L'évolution de la societé du Bahrain.' Thèse pour le doctorat, Faculté des Lettres et Sciences Humaines, Sorbonne, Université de Paris, 1970.
904. United Nations Development Program. 'A Preliminary Investigation into the Social Situation and Needs of Women in Villages in Bahrain.' New York: U.N.D.P., 1976.
905. United Nations Development Program. 'Preliminary Investigation into the Social Situation and Needs of Women in Villages in Bahrain. Project Findings and Recommendations' (DP/UN/BAH–73–009/1). New York: U.N.D.P., 1977.

EGYPT

906. Abd Al-Razik, Ahmad. *La femme au temps des Mamlouks en Egypte.* Textes Arabes et Etudes Islamiques. Le Caire: Institut Français d'Archéologie Orientale du Caire, 1973.
907. Abdel Fateh, Kamilia. 'Children of Working Mothers.' Ph.D. dissertation, Ein Shams University, Egypt, 1968.
908. Abdel Fattah, al Sayyid. *De l'étendue des droits de la femme dans le mariage musulman et particulièrement en Egypte.* Paris, 1922.
909. Abdel Kader, Soha. 'Conservative and Modern Egyptian Family Types.' Paper presented at the 3rd Workshop on Family and Kinship sponsored by Kuwait University and UNESCO, Kuwait, 27–30 Nov., 1976.

910. Abdel Kader, Soha. *The Status of Egyptian Women, 1900–1973.* Cairo: Ford Foundation, 1973.
911. Abdul Qayyum, Shah. 'Women in West Asia: a Case Study of Egypt.' *Islam and the Modern Age* 4, 3 (1973):54–83.
912. Abou Zeid, Hekmat *et al. The Education of Women in the U.A.R. During the 19th and 20th Centuries.* Paris: UNESCO Publications, 1970.
913. Abu Lughod, Janet and Amin, Lucy. 'Egyptian Marriage Advertisements: Microcosm of a Changing Society.' *Journal of Marriage and Family Living* 23, 2 (1961): 127–36.
914. Adams, John Boman. 'Culture and Conflict in an Egyptian Village.' *American Anthropologist* no. 59 (Apr. 1957):225–35.
915. Afro-Asian People's Solidarity Organization. Permanent Secretariat. *Comparative Studies in the Legal Rights of Women in Africa and Asia, particularly in Egypt.* Cairo, 1972.
916. Aliyah, Muhammad Kamil el Bindary. 'A Cultural Approach to Nursing Education in the UAR.' Ph.D. dissertation, Boston University, 1965.
917. Amine, R.G. *Seven Years in the Sun.* London: Robert Hale, 1959.
918. Arafa, Bahiga. *The Social Activities of the Egyptian Feminist Union.* Cairo: Eltas Modern Press, 1954.
919. Arnett, Mary Flounders. 'Qasim Amin and the Beginning of the Feminist Movement in Egypt.' Ph.D. dissertation, Dropsie University, Philadelphia, 1966.
920. Babazogli, S. *L'éducation de la jeune fille musulmane en Egypte.* Cairo: Barbey, 1928.
921. Badran, Hoda. 'Population and Development: Egyptian Women's Perspective.' Beirut: UNICEF, n.d.
922. Badran, Margot. 'Institution of Harim and Aspects of Harim Life in the late 19th and early 20th Century Egypt.' Paper presented at the 8th Middle East Studies Association Annual Meeting, Boston, 6–9 Nov., 1974.
923. Le Balle, R. 'La condition privée de la femme égyptienne

musulmane.' *L'Egypte Contemporaine* 24, 141 (1933):415–434.

924. Balley, C. 'Bedouin Weddings in Sinai and the Negev.' *Folklore Research Center Studies* 4 (1974):105–132.

925. El Baymoumi, Soheir. 'Health and Illness as Indices of Sex Status in an Egyptian Village.' Paper presented at the 75th Annual Meeting of the American Anthropological Association, Washington, D.C., 17–21 Nov., 1976.

926. Bayyuni, Muhammed Ahmed Muhammad. 'The Islamic Ethnic of Social Justice and the Spirit of Modernization. An Application of Weber's Thesis to the Relationship Between Religious Values and Social Change in Modern Egypt.' Ph.D. dissertation, Temple University, 1976.

927. Bindary, Aziza, Bexter, Colin B. and Hollingsworth, T.H. 'Urban Rural Differences in the Relationship Between Women's Employment and Fertility: a Preliminary Study.' *Journal of Biosocial Science* no. 5 (1973):159–67.

928. Bohdanowicz, Arslan. 'The Feminist Movement in Egypt.' *Islamic Review* 39 (Aug. 1951):26–33.

929. Cairo Family Planning Association. Seminar on the Legal Status of Women in the Family and its Effect on their Attitudes towards Childbearing. Cairo, 14–16 Feb., 1978. *WIN News* 4 (Summer 1978): 40–41.

930. el-Calamawy, Suhair. 'Women Win their Way to Higher Public Posts.' *Times* (London), July 1969.

931. Carol, Jacqueline. *Cocktails and Camels.* New York: Appleton-Century-Crofts, 1960.

932. 'Changes in the Social Role of the Egyptian Woman.' Research project in progress sponsored by the National Center for Social and Criminological Research, Cairo, Egypt.

933. Charaoui, G. 'L'évolution du féminisme en Egypte.' *Voix des Humbles* (Dec. 1934):1.

934. Columbia Human Rights Law Review. Columbia University School of Law, eds. *Law and the Status of Women. An International Symposium.* New York:

United Nations, Center for Social Development and Humanitarian Affairs, 1977.

935. Contu, Giuseppe. 'Le donne comuniste e il movimento democratico femminile in Egitto fino al 1965.' *Oriente Moderno* 55, 5 (May–June 1975):237–247.

936. Cooper, Elizabeth. *The Women of Egypt*. London: Hurst and Blackett, 1914.

937. Debs, Richard Abraham. 'The Law of Property in Egypt: Islamic Law and Civil Code.' Ph.D. dissertation, Princeton University, 1963.

938. Dodd, Peter. 'Youth and Women's Emancipation in the United Arab Republic.' *Middle East Journal* 22 (Spring 1968):159–172.

939. 'Donna: parere di el-Azhar sulla funzione della donna nella società.' *Oriente Moderno* 36, 5 (1956):351.

940. Douglas, Joseph and Douglas, K.W. 'Aspects of Marriage and Family Living among Egyptian Peasants.' *Marriage and Family Living* 16 (1954):45–8.

941. 'A Draft Law Giving the Egyptian Woman the Right to Sue for Divorce.' *New York Times*, 6 Mar. 1976. (Also in *Women's International Network News* 2, 2 (Spring 1976):39.)

942. 'Egypt: Cairo Family Planning Association.' *WIN News* 2 (Summer 1976):35.

943. Egypt. International Women's Year Committee. 'The Relations Between Education, Training and National Development.' 1975.

944. Egypt. International Women's Year. National Status of Women's Committee. 'A General Survey of Status of Women in Egypt in Legislation. Prepared by the Legislation Committee.' (Mimeographed.)

945. 'Egypt: Interview with Aziza Hussein.' *WIN News* 3 (Spring 1977):44–46.

946. 'Egypt: Jobs for the Girls.' *The Economist* 8 Apr., 1974, p. 44.

947. Egypt. Ministry of National Guidance. *The Role of Women in the United Arab Republic*. Cairo: Ministry of National Guidance, 1965.

948. *Egyptian Laws Related to Marriage, Family and Personal Status*. Beirut, Dar el Fikr Al-Arabi, 1977.

949. 'Egyptian Women Attuned to the 20th Century.' *Arab World* 12, 12 (1966).

950. 'Equality: Egypt.' *WIN News* 2 (Spring 1976):39.

951. Esposito, John L. 'Muslim Family Law in Egypt and Pakistan: a Critical Analysis of Legal Reform, its Sources and Methodological Problems.' Ph.D. dissertation, Temple University, 1974.

952. Fahmy, Hoda. 'Changing Women in a Changing Society: a Study of Emergent Consciousness of Young Women in the City of Akhmin in Upper Egypt.' M.A. thesis, Department of Sociology/Anthropology/Psychology, American University of Cairo, 1978.

953. Fakhouri, Hani. 'The Zar Cult in an Egyptian Village.' *Anthropological Quarterly* 41 (1968):49–56.

954. Farrag, A.M. 'Remarriages, Multiple Marriages and Polygamous Nuptuality Tables in the U.A.R.— 1960.' In *International Population Conference, London* (1969):2180–2181.

955. Fergany, Nader. 'Egyptian Women and National Development, a Demographic Background.' Paper presented at a Seminar on Arab Women in National Development, sponsored by UNICEF, Arab League and Arab States Adult Functional Literacy Center, Cairo, Egypt, 24–30 Sept., 1972.

956. Fernea, Robert. *Nubians in Egypt, Peaceful People.* Austin: University of Texas Press, 1977.

957. Geargoura, Christian M. 'Women's Prison: Cohesion and Social Structure: a Study of Qanater Women's Prison.' M.A. thesis, American University of Cairo, 1969.

958. Gharzouzi, Eva. 'The Demographic Aspects of Women's Employment in the United Arab Republic.' Paper presented at the Conference of the International Union for the Scientific Study of Population, London, Sept. 1969. (Also in *Egyptian Population and Family Planning Review* 3, 2 (1970):93–98.)

959. Giele, Janet Z. and Smock, A.C. *Women: Roles and*

Status in Eight Countries. New York: John Wiley, 1977.

960. Gornick, Vivian. *In Search of Ali Mahmoud: an American Woman in Egypt.* New York: Saturday Review Press, 1973.

961. Granada-Dewey, Judith. 'Interim Report: Women and Health in Egypt.' Paper presented at the United Nations World Conference for the International Women's Year, Mexico City, 19 June–2 July, 1975.

962. Greiss, Syada Elhamy. 'The Role of Women and Attitudes to Family Size.' Thesis, Faculty of Social Anthropology, American University of Cairo, Egypt, 1971.

963. Haikal, Ayten. 'Some Managerial Problems of Female Employment in the United Arab Republic.' M.A. thesis, American University of Cairo, Egypt, 1971.

964. El-Hamamsy, Leila S. 'The Changing Role of the Egyptian Woman.' *Middle East Forum* 33, 6 (1958): 24–28.

965. El-Hamamsy, Leila S. 'The "Daya" of Egypt: Survival in a Modernizing Society.' Cal. Tech. Population Program, Occasional Papers Series 1, no. 8, 1973.

966. Hansen, H.H. 'Clitoridectomy: Female Circumcision in Egypt.' *Folk* 14–15 (1972/73).

967. Holtzclaw, Katherine. 'Extension Service for Farm Girls and Women of the UAR.' End of Tour Report, USAID/UAR, 1964.

968. Horis, S. 'My Impression of Egyptian Women: Part I.' (In Japanese.) *Chûtô-tsûhô*, 246 (Feb. 1977):21–36.

969. Hussein, Aziza. 'The Family as a Social Unit—Responsibilities of Husband and Wife.' Paper presented at the 8th Conference of the International Planned Parenthood Federation, Santiago, Chile, Apr. 1967.

970. Hussein, Aziza. 'Helping Egypt's Women to Help Themselves.' *Unesco Features* (Nos. 676/677/678/, 1975):39–42.

971. Hussein, Aziza. 'Recent Developments in the United Arab Republic—Symposium on Birth Control and the Changing Status of Women.' Paper presented at the United Nations 50th Anniversary Conference

on the Population Crisis: 20th Century Challenge, New York, Oct. 1966.

972. Hussein, Aziza. 'The Role of Women in Social Reform in Egypt.' *Middle East Journal* 7 (1953):440–450.

973. Hussein, Aziza. 'Status of Women and Family Planning in a Developing Country—Egypt.' Paper presented at the 4th International Teach-In Conference on Exploding Humanity, Toronto University, Toronto, Nov. 1968.

974. Hussein, Aziza. 'The Status of Women in Family Law in the United Arab Republic.' Paper presented at the Seminar on the Status of Women in Family Law, Lomé, Togo, 18–31 Aug., 1964. (Seminar organized by the UN Commission on the Status of Women.)

975. Hussein, Aziza and Abdel Hamid, Najib. 'Report on Egypt.' Paper presented at the Regional Conference on Education, Vocational Training and Work Opportunities for Girls and Women in African Countries, sponsored by the UN Economic Commission for Africa and the German Foundation for Developing Countries, Rabat, Morocco, 20–29 May, 1971. (Mimeographed.)

976. Hussein, P.H. 'Endogamy in Egyptian Nubia.' *Journal of Biosocial Science* 3, 3 (1971):251–257.

977. International Women's Year. Legislation Committee. 'A General Survey of the Status of Women in Egypt in Legislation.' Paper presented at the United Nations World Conference for the International Women's Year, Mexico City, 19 June–2 July, 1975.

978. Kennedy, J.G. 'Nubian Zar Ceremonies as Psychotherapy.' *Human Organization* 26 (1967):280–285.

979. Khalifa, Ahmed M. *Status of Women in Relation to Fertility and Family Planning in Egypt*. Cairo: National Center for Sociological and Criminological Research, 1973.

980. Krachkovsky, I.Y. 'Kasim Amin, Sovetnik appellyatsionnogo suda. Novaya zhenshchina. Perevod so 2-go arabskogo izdaniya i predislovie.' *Mir Islama* 1 (1912):119.

981. Lane, E.W. *Manners and Customs of the Modern Egyptians.* London: Everyman's Library, 1860. (Reprinted 1954.)

982. 'The Legal Status of Women in Egypt.' Cairo, 1975. (Pamphlet.)

983. Lichtenstadter, Ilse. 'An Arab Egyptian Family.' *Middle East Journal* 6, 4 (1952):379–399.

984. Lichtenstadter, Ilse. 'The Muslim Woman in Transition, Based on Observations in Egypt and Pakistan.' *Sociologus* 7, 1 (1957):23–28.

985. Lichtenstadter, Ilse. 'The New Woman in Modern Egypt.' *Muslim World* 38 (1948):163–171.

986. Maghraby, Marlene. 'Zamala, Sadaka and Conceptions of Relations Between the Sexes among Urban Cairo Youth and Adults.' M.A. thesis, American University of Cairo, Egypt, 1973.

987. Manniche, L. 'Some Aspects of Ancient Egyptian Sexual Life.' *Acta Orientalia* 38 (1977):11–24.

988. Merriam, Kathleen Howard. 'The Impact of Educational Experiences upon the Professional and Public Careers of Contemporary Egyptian Women.' Paper presented at the Wellesley Conference on Women and Development, Wellesley College, Mass., 2–6 June, 1976.

989. Merriam, Kathleen Howard. 'The Impact of Modern Secular Education upon Egyptian Women's Participation in Public Life.' Paper presented at the 10th Middle East Studies Association Annual Meeting, Los Angeles, 10–13 Nov., 1976.

990. Miéville, W. 'The Fellah's Yokemate.' *Fortnightly Review* 85 (1906):1093–1105.

991. Mitchel, Loretta A. 'The Sorrow of Egypt.' *Muslim World* 3 (1913): 64–66.

992. Mito, Mohammad Abdel Moneim S. 'The Social Change of Daughters' Position in Egyptian Moslem Middle Class Families in Alexandria.' Thesis, Institute of Sociology and Social Science, Alexandria University, Egypt, 1953.

993. 'Model suffragette.' *Newsweek*, 22 June, 1953, p. 44.

994. Mohamed, Hafez Mohamed. 'The Level of Fertility of the Married Female Employee in Major Marketing Organizations in Cairo.' Cairo, Egypt, June 1965.

995. Al-Mu'tasim, M. 'The Education of Females in Modern Egypt.' Ph.D. dissertation, Manchester University, 1954.

996. Nabraoui, C. 'L'évolution du féminisme en Egypte.' *L'Egyptienne* no. 2 (March 1925):40–46.

997. Nabraoui, C. 'Le mouvement féministe en Egypte.' *L'Egyptienne* no. 5 (June 1925):159–163.

998. Nabraoui, C. 'Les progrès de l'enseignement des jeunes filles en Egypte.' *L'Egyptienne* no. 55 (Dec. 1928): 2–8.

999. Nabraoui, C. 'Le statut juridique de la femme egyptienne.' *L'Egyptienne* no. 66 (1931):3–16.

1000. Nadim, Nawal el-Messiri. 'Family Relationships in a "Harah" in Cairo.' Paper presented at the 3rd Workshop on Family and Kinship sponsored by Kuwait University and UNESCO, Kuwait, 27–30 Nov., 1976.

1001. Nadim, Nawal el-Messiri. 'Support Systems Involving Widows in the City of Cairo.' Research project in progress sponsored by the Department of Health, Education and Welfare, Social Research Center, American University of Cairo, Egypt.

1002. Nagi, Moustafa H. 'Demographic and Socio-Economic Analysis of the Egyptian Labor Force 1937–1965.' Ph.D. dissertation, University of Connecticut, 1970.

1003. Nagi, Moustafa H. *Labor Force and Employment in Egypt: a Demographic and Socioeconomic Analysis.* New York: Praeger, 1971.

1004. Nallino, C.A. 'Opera e domande dell'associazione per l'unione femminile egiziana, e considerazione d'un qadi sulle domande dell'associazione per l'unione femminile egiziana.' (Activities and Demands of the Egyptian Women's Union. The Comments of a Qadi.) *Oriente Moderno* 6, 6 (1926):339–342.

1005. Nelson, Cynthia. 'Changing Roles of Men and Women: Illustrations from Egypt.' *Anthropological Quarterly* 41, 2 (1968):57–77.

1006. Nelson, Cynthia. 'Self, Spirit Possession and World View: an Illustration from Egypt.' *International Journal of Social Psychiatry* 17 (1971):194–209.

1007. Nerval, G. de. 'Les femmes du Caire.' *Revue des Deux Mondes* (May/July/Sept. 1846).

1008. Northcott, L.C. 'Egyptian Women and the Changing Times.' *Independent Woman* 35 (Sept. 1956):4–5.

1009. Palmer, M.R. 'As-Sufur—"The Unveiled": a Weekly Newspaper for Moslem Women.' *Muslim World* 8 (1918):168–171.

1010. Perlmann, M. 'Women and Feminism in Egypt.' *Palestine Affairs* 4 (March 1949):36–39.

1011. Petersen, Karen Kay. 'Family and Kin in Contemporary Egypt.' Ph.D. dissertation, Columbia University, 1967.

1012. Phillips, Daisy Griggs. 'The Awakening of Egypt's Womanhood.' *Muslim World* 18, 1 (1928):402–408.

1013. Phillips, Daisy Griggs. 'The Growth of the Feminist Movement in Egypt.' *Muslim World* 16, 3 (1926): 277–285.

1014. Pierre, R. 'L'évolution de la femme musulmane en Egypte.' *En Terre d'Islam* (1933):277–287, 297–310.

1015. Rashed, Fatma Minet. 'Egypt's Women Win their Rights.' *UN World* 5 (Mar. 1951):72–74.

1016. Rasheed, Bahega S. *The Egyptian Feminist Union.* Cairo: Anglo-Egyptian Bookshop, 1973.

1017. Rodriguez Mellado, I. 'Notas sobre la evolución social de la mujer egipcia.' *Cuadernos de Estudios Africanos* 17 (1952):49–62.

1018. Ross, Mary. 'The Calioub Home Economics Extension Program for Rural Women in Egypt.' *Fundamental and Adult Education* 8, 3 (1956):98–105.

1019. Rossi, E. 'Discussioni e polemiche in Egitto sull'-ugualianza tra l'uomo e la donna.' (Discussions and Polemics in Egypt about Equality Between Men and Women.) *Oriente Moderno* 10, 6 (1930):284–285.

1020. Rossi, E. 'L'unione femminile egiziana chiede al governo l'abolizione della poligamia. Polemiche e contrasti.' (The Egyptian Women's Union Asks the

Government to Abolish Polygamy. Polemics and Contrasts.) *Oriente Moderno* 15, 9 (1935):476–478.

1021. Rossi, E. 'L'unione femminile egiziana ed il congresso dell'alleanza femminile internazionale a Roma—echi del congresso femminile internazionale di Roma—deliberazioni del comitato dell'unione femminile egiziana dopo il congresso di Roma.' (Egyptian Women Call for their Rights, Especially in Matters of Education and Marriage, at the Congress of the International Women's Alliance in Rome.) *Oriente Moderno* 3, 6 (1923):376–379.

1022. Rushdi Pacha, Mme (Niya Salima). *Harems et musulmanes d'Egypte*. Paris: Félix Juven, n.d.

1023. Sabri, Munira. 'The Girl Guide Movement.' *Education Bureau Bulletin* no. 29 (Oct. 1948):4–5.

1024. Sadat, Jihan. 'The Role of First Lady.' *Egypt Today* no. 1 (May 1976):16–18.

1025. Sakakini, Doria. 'Egypt's Peasant Women.' *Muslim World* 35, 1 (1952):32–43.

1026. Saleh, Saneya. 'Professional Women and National Development: Women's Response to Migration.' Paper presented at the Open University Women Seminar Series of Women, Work and Social Change, American University of Cairo, Cairo, Egypt, 16 May, 1977.

1027. El Samman, Mohammad Issa. 'La scolarisation des garçons et des filles en Haute-Egypte (Qena).' Doctorat d'Université, Paris University, Faculty of Education, 1976.

1028. El Shamy, Hassan. 'Mental Health in Traditional Culture: a Study of Preventive and Therapeutic Folk Practices in Egypt.' *Catalyst* 6 (1972):13–28.

1029. Saunders, Lucie W. 'Women, Men and Political Power in an Egyptian Village.' Paper presented at the 9th Annual Middle East Studies Association Meeting, Louisville, Ky., 19–22 Nov., 1975.

1030. El-Sawi, Shahera. *The Nubian Woman in Cairo, Patterns of Adjustments: a Case Study of Five Families*. Cairo: American University of Cairo, 1965.

1031. Shafik, Doria (Shafik, Doria Ragai). 'Egyptian Feminism.' *Middle East Affairs* 3 (1952):233–238.
1032. Shafik, Doria (Shafik, Doria Ragai). *The Egyptian Woman.* Cairo, 1955.
1033. Shafik, Doria (Shafik, Doria Ragai). *La femme nouvelle en Egypte.* Le Caire, 1944.
1034. Shafik, Doria (Shafik, Doria Ragai). *La femme et le droit religieux de l'Egypte contemporaine.* Paris: Paul Geuthner, 1940.
1035. Shafik, Doria (Shafik, Doria Ragai). 'Les revendications politiques de la femme egyptienne.' *Articles et Documents de la Bibliothèque de la Documentation Française* (19 May 1949).
1036. Sherbini, Isabel. 'Working Paper on Egypt.' Paper presented at the United Nations Seminar on the Participation of Women in Economic Life, Libreville, Gabon, July–Aug., 1971.
1037. Sidhom, Samiha. 'Emancipation of Women as a Social Movement in Egypt.' *National Review of Social Sciences* 3, 1 (Jan. 1966):95–135.
1038. Siham, B. *Frauenbildung und Frauenbewegung in Ägypten.* (Education of Women and Women's Movements in Egypt.) Wuppertal: Kölner Arbeiten zur Pädagogik, 1968.
1039. Soueif, M.I. 'The Changing Role of Women in Contemporary Egypt.' *National Review of Social Sciences* 12, 2–3 (Sept. 1975):1–20.
1040. Sourial, Aida Fahmy. 'The Hakima: a Study on the Socialization of a Professional Role.' M.A. thesis, American University of Cairo, Egypt, 1969.
1041. 'The Status of Women: Egypt.' *WIN News* 4 (Winter 1978):82.
1042. Stillman, Yedida K. 'The Importance of the Cairo Geniza Manuscripts for the History of Medieval Female Attire.' *International Journal of Middle East Studies* 7, 4 (1976):579–589. (Based on the author's doctoral dissertation 'Female Attire of Medieval Egypt: According to the Trousseau Lists and Cognate Material from the Cairo Geniza,' University of Pennsylvania, 1972.)

1043. Sukkary, Suheir. 'A Report on Women and Education in Egypt: a Case Study of Vocational Education in an Egyptian Village.'

1044. Suleiman, Michael W. 'Changing Attitudes Toward Women in Egypt: the Role of Fiction in Women's Magazines.' Kansas: Kansas State University, n.d. (Also presented as a paper at the 8th Annual Middle East Studies Association Meeting, Boston, 6–9 Nov., 1974.)

1045. Thompson, A.Y. 'The Woman Question in Egypt.' *Muslim World* 4 (1914):266–272.

1046. Tillion, Germaine. 'Women in Egypt: Towards Equality.' *World Health*, Sept.–Oct. 1969, pp. 2–11.

1047. Timm, Klaus and Aalami, S. *Die Muslimische Frau zwischen Tradition und Fortschritt: Frauenfrage und Familien-entwicklung in Ägypten und Iran*. Berlin: Akademie Verlag, 1976.

1048. Tomiche, Nada. 'Changing Status of Egyptian Women.' *New Outlook* 1 (Sept. 1957):39–40.

1049. Tomiche, Nada. 'La condition de la femme dans le Moyen Orient arabe.' *Documentation Française, Notes et Etudes, Série Sociale* 54, 150 (1955). (Also in *Journal of Near East Studies* 17 (1958):90.)

1050. Tomiche, Nada. 'La femme dans l'Egypte moderne.' *Etudes Méditerranéennes* (Summer 1957):99–111.

1051. Tomiche, Nada. 'The Position of Women in the UAR.' *Journal of Contemporary History* 3, 3 (1968):129–143.

1052. Vacca, V. 'L'unione femminile egiziana domanda al presidente del consiglio numerose riformi sociali.' (The Egyptian Women's Union Asks for Many Social Reforms.) *Oriente Moderno* 16, 5 (1936):295–296.

1053. Vaucher-Zananiri, Nelly. 'Le rôle des femmes dans la RAU.' *Preuves-Informations* 16 (3 Jan., 1961).

1054. Veccia-Vaglieri, L. 'Movimento femminista egiziano.' (Egyptian Feminist Movement.) *Oriente Moderno* 16, 9 (1936):530–531.

1055. Vial, C. 'Le roman égyptian depuis la seconde guerre mondiale.' *Annales Islamologiques* 7 (1967):97–119.

1056. Waddy, Charles. 'Egypt's Modern Women—the First Fifty Years.' *Middle East International* no. 24 (June 1973):30–31.
1057. Wanner, L. 'L'évolution de la femme dans l'Islam moderne.' *L'Egyptienne* (1939):21.
1058. Wasfi, Atif Amin. 'The Changing Family in Three Egyptian Villages.' Paper presented at the 3rd Workshop on Family and Kinship sponsored by Kuwait University and UNESCO, Kuwait, 27–30 Nov., 1976.
1059. Wenig, Steffen. *Women in Egyptian Art.* New York: McGraw-Hill, 1970.
1060. Williams, Neil Vincent. 'Factory Employment and Family Relations in an Egyptian Village.' Ph.D. dissertation, University of Michigan, Ann Arbor, 1964.
1061. Winkel, Annegret. *Jihan el Sadat: First Lady und Frauenrechtlerin am Nil.* Koblenz: Gorres-Verlag, 1976.
1062. *Women and Higher Education.* Cairo. (Pamphlet.)
1063. *Women and Culture in Egypt.* Cairo. (Pamphlet.)
1064. Work, Margaret. 'Egypt's Peasant Women.' *Muslim World* 35 (1945):32–43.
1065. Ziadé, M. 'Il risveglio della donna in Egitto negli ultimi cento anni.' (The Revival of the Egyptian Woman in the Last Hundred Years.) *Oriente Moderno* 9, 5 (1929):236–248.

IRAQ

1066. Abbott, Nabia. *Two Queens of Baghdad: Mother and Wife of Harun.* Chicago: University of Chicago Press, 1946.
1067. Anderson, J.N.D. 'A Law of Personal Status for Iraq.' *International Comparative Law Quarterly* 9 (1966): 542–563.

1068. Baali, F. 'Educational Aspirations among College Girls in Iraq.' *Sociology and Social Research* 51, 4 (July 1967):485–93.

1069. Barth, Fredrik. 'Father's Brother's Daughter Marriage in Kurdistan.' *Southwest Journal of Anthropology* 10 (1954):164–171.

1070. El-Bustan, Afifa I. 'Problems Facing a Selected Group of Iraqi Women.' Ph.D. dissertation, Columbia University, 1956.

1071. Butti, Rufail. 'La donna irachena moderna.' (The Modern Iraqi Woman.) *Oriente Moderno* 28 (Apr.–June 1948):108–112.

1072. Drower, E.S. 'Woman and Taboo in Iraq.' *Iraq Journal* 5 (1938):105–116.

1073. Fernea, Elizabeth. *Guests of the Sheikh: an Ethnography of an Iraqi Village.* New York: Doubleday, 1969.

1074. Fernea, Robert A. *Shaykh and Effendi: Changing Patterns of Authority among the El Shabana of Southern Iraq.* Cambridge, Mass.: Harvard University Press, 1970.

1075. General Federation of Iraqi Women. 'Work Programme of the Preparatory Committee for the International Women's Year 1975. Emanated from the General Federation of Iraqi Women.' (Mimeographed.)

1076. Hansen, Henry H. *The Kurdish Woman's Life: Field Research in a Muslim Society, Iraq.* Leiden: Brill, 1961.

1077. Iraq. Ministry of Social Affairs and Labour. *The Scientific and Technological Influence on the Woman and the Family in Iraq.* Jan. 1969.

1078. El-Kassir, Maliha. 'The Effect of Civilization Factors on Iraqi Family Planning and Family Size.' Paper presented at the 3rd Workshop on Family and Kinship, sponsored by Kuwait University and UNESCO, Kuwait, 27–30 Nov., 1976.

1079. El-Kassir, Maliha. 'Role of Women in the Development of Iraqi Society.' Research project in progress sponsored by the Department of Sociology, University of Baghdad, Iraq.

1080. El-Kassir, Maliha. 'The Woman's Status in Modern Iraq.' Baghdad, 1965.
1081. El-Kassir, Maliha. 'Women and the Family and their Role in Economic Development.' Paper presented at the Seminar on Women and Social Development, Baghdad, Iraq, 28 Dec., 1975.
1082. Khayyat, Latif. 'Judeo-Iraqi Proverbs on Man and Wife.' *Proverbium* 24 (1974):943–947.
1083. De Marchi, M. *et al.* 'Food Consumption and Nutrition Status of Pregnant Women Attending a Maternal and Child Health Center in Baghdad.' *Journal of the Faculty of Medicine* (Baghdad) no. 8 (1966).
1084. Qadry, Hind Tahsin. 'Problems of Women Teachers in Iraq.' Ph.D. dissertation, Stanford University, 1957.
1085. Rahmatallah, Malleeha. 'The Women of Baghdad in the 9th and 10th Century as Revealed in the History of Baghdad of Al-Hatib.' M.A. thesis, University of Pennsylvania, 1963.
1086. Vacca, V. 'Il congresso femminile di Baghdad.' (The Women's Congress at Baghdad.) *Oriente Moderno* 12, 11 (1932):525.
1087. 'Women's Development—Iraq.' *WIN News* 4, 2 (Spring 1978):67.
1088. Yasseen, Shahzanan. 'Educational Opportunities for Women in Iraq.' Paper presented at the International Alliance of Women, Copenhagen, 28 July– 24 Aug., 1954.

JORDAN

1089. Anderson, J.N.D. 'The Jordanian Law of Family Rights.' *Muslim World* (1952):190–206.
1090. Barhoum, Mohammad Issa. *Divorce and the Status of Women in Jordan.* Amman: Scientific Research Council, n.d.
1091. Barhoum, Mohammad Issa. 'The Marriage System in a

Jordanian Village: Jabir.' Paper presented at the 3rd Workshop on Family and Kinship, sponsored by the Kuwait University and UNESCO, Kuwait, 27–30 Nov., 1976.

1092. 'Le code des droits de la famille de la Jordanie.' *Oriente Moderno* 50, 1–2 (Jan.–Feb. 1970):1–11.

1093. Hirabayashi, Gordon K. 'Social Change in Jordan: A Quantitative Approach in a Non-Census Area.' *American Journal of Sociology* 64, 1 (1958):36–40.

1094. 'Jordan: Department of Women's Affairs.' *Women at Work* (ILO) no. 3 (1977):3.

1095. Jordan. Ministry of Labor. Department of Women's Affairs. 'The Role of Mass Media in Attracting Women for Employment.' (A Study of the Image of Woman as Presented in Different Mass Communication Media in Jordan.) Amman, 4–7 Apr., 1976.

1096. Jordan. Ministry of Labor. Department of Women's Affairs. A Working Paper Setting Forth the Aims and Functions of the Department, by Ina'm al-Mufti, Director of the Department. Amman, June 1977.

1097. 'Jordan: Na'ur Ladies Organization.' *WIN News* 2 (Summer 1976):36.

1098. Kandis, Afaf Deab. 'Female Education and Fertility Decline in a Developing Country: the Case of Jordan.' *Population Bulletin of the United Nations Economic Commission for Western Asia* no. 13 (July 1977):17–31.

1099. Khayo, Mary. 'A Survey of Vocational Training Opportunities for Girls in Jordan and Recommendations Concerning Vocations in Home Economics.' Paper presented for partial fulfillment of B.A. degree at the Beirut College for Women, 1964.

1100. Khayri, Majduddin Omar. 'Attitudes Toward the Changing Role of Women in Jordan: a Study of University Graduates.' M.A. thesis, American University of Beirut, Lebanon, Oct. 1975.

1101. Khayri, Majduddin Omar. 'Working Women in Technical and Professional Jobs in Jordan.' Research project in progress sponsored by the Department of Sociology, University of Jordan, Amman, Jordan, 1976.

1102. Lunt, James. 'Love in the Desert.' *Blackwood's Magazine* 278 (1955):333–339.

1103. Lutfiyya, Abdulla M. *Baytin: a Jordanian Village*. The Hague: Mouton, 1966.

1104. El-Mufty, E. 'Scholarship that Brought Tears.' *UN Review* 4 (May 1958):20–21.

1105. Mallah, M.A., ed. *The Role of the Jordanian Woman*. (Proceedings of the Second Symposium on Manpower Development.) Amman, Jordan, 4–7 Apr., 1976.

1106. Nasir, Sari J. 'Working Women in the Changing Society of Jordan.' *Faculty of Arts Journal* (Jordan University) 1, 2 (1969):7–41.

1107. *Perspective—Jordan's Magazine for Women. An Independent Non-Political Monthly Magazine for and about Women in the Arab World.*

1108. Qutub, Ishaq. 'The Rise of the Middle Class in Jordan.' *Middle East Forum* (Dec. 1961):40–44.

1109. Rizk, Hanna. 'Trends in Fertility and Family Planning in Jordan.' *Studies in Family Planning* 8 (Apr. 1977):91–99.

1110. Es-Said, Nimra Tannous (Tannous, Nimra). 'The Changing Role of Women in Jordan: a Threat or an Asset?' Paper presented to the Research Committee on Sex Roles in Society, 8th World Congress of Sociology, Toronto, 1974.

1111. Es-Said, Nimra Tannous (Tannous, Nimra). 'New Horizons: a Study on Emancipation of Women of Jordan.' Amman: UN and Jordanian Ministry of Social Affairs, n.d.

1112. Es-Said, Nimra Tannous (Tannous, Nimra). 'Part-time Work for Women.' Paper presented at a seminar on Development of Human Resources, The Role of Women in Jordan, Jordan, 1975.

1113. Es-Said, Nimra Tannous (Tannous, Nimra). 'The Role of Women in Jordan.' Paper presented at the International Women's Congress, Madrid, June 1970.

1114. Es-Said, Nimra Tannous (Tannous, Nimra). 'Women and Development in Jordan: a Challenge for Partnership.' Paper presented at the 3rd Workshop on Family and Kinship, sponsored by Kuwait University and UNESCO, Kuwait, 27–30 Nov., 1976.
1115. Turing, Penelope. 'Women in Jordan: Progress and Participation.' *Middle East International* (June 1976):20–22.

KUWAIT

1116. Calverley, Eleanor J. *My Arabian Days and Nights.* New York: Thomas Y. Crowell Co., 1958.
1117. Chelhod, Joseph. 'Notes sur le mariage chez les arabes au Kuwait.' *Journal de la Société des Africanistes* 26 (1956):255–62.
1118. Dickson, H.R.P. *The Arab of the Desert: a Glimpse into Badawin Life in Kuwait and Saudi Arabia.* London: Allen and Unwin, 1949.
1119. Dickson, Violet. *Forty Years in Kuwait.* London: Allen and Unwin, 1971.
1120. 'The Evolution that Feeds Kuwait's Daughters.' *Kuwait Digest* (Apr.–June 1975):8–15.
1121. Fletcher, David. 'Drawing a Veil on Classroom Life.' *Sunday Telegraph* (London), 14 July, 1974.
1122. Freeth, Zahra (Dickson). *Kuwait was my Home.* New York: Macmillan, 1956.
1123. 'A Hit with the Misses: inside the University College for Women.' *Kuwait Digest* 5, 2 (Apr.–June 1977): 22–24.
1124. Kuwait. Central Statistics Office. 'Appointment of Kuwaiti Women Graduates in the Financial Year 1969–1970.' Kuwait, 1970.
1125. Kuwait. Family Development Society. Research Studies

and Information Committee. *March of the Kuwaiti Women in 11 Years Through the Family Development Society, n.d.* Translated by F.Y. Shihab. Kuwait, 1974.

1126. Kuwait. Ministère des Affaires Sociales et du Travail. Bureau de Planification. *Le statut de la femme au Koweit* (July 1964).

1127. Kuwait. Ministry of Education. 'Access of Young Girls and Women to Technical and Vocational Education in Kuwait.' Kuwait, 1969.

1128. Kuwait. Ministry of Education. *Reports on Girls and Women Education.* 1968.

1129. Kuwait. Ministry of Social Affairs and Labour. *Report to the Secretary-General of U.N. on the Scientific and Technological Progress on the Status of Women Workers in Kuwait,* Apr. 1969.

1130. Kuwait. Permanent Mission of the State of Kuwait to the UN. *Kuwaiti Women and International Women's Year.* Booklet. (Résumé available in *WIN News* 1, 4 (Oct. 1975):60.)

1131. Meleis, Afaf. 'Changing Roles and Self Concepts among Kuwaiti Women.' Paper presented at the Symposium of Near Eastern Women through the Ages, Berkeley, Calif., 1975.

1132. Nath, Kamla. 'Education and Employment among Kuwaiti Women.' 1974. (Mimeographed, c/o UNDP, P.O. Box 1011, Freetown, Sierra Leone.)

1133. Stuers, Cora Vreede-de. 'Girl Students in Kuwait.' *Bijdragen tot de Taal- Land- en Volkenkunde* 130, 1 (1974):110–131.

1134. Al-Thakeb, Fahad T. 'The Status of Women in Contemporary Kuwaiti Society.' Research project in progress sponsored by the Department of Sociology and Social Work, Kuwait University, Kuwait.

1135. 'Women's Lib.—Kuwait Style.' *Middle East* (May 1978):78.

LEBANON

1136. Abu Khadra, Rihab. 'Recent Changes in Lebanese Moslem Marriages Shown by Changes in Marriage Contracts.' M.A. thesis, American University of Beirut, Lebanon, 1959.

1137. Abu Nasr, J. 'Women Employment in Lebanon.' Paper presented at the Career Counselling Conference (Far Eastern Conferences). Tokyo, Ehwa and New Delhi, May 1978.

1138. Accad-Sursock, R. 'La femme libanaise: de la tradition à la modernité.' *Travaux et Jours* 52 (July–Sept. 1974):17–38.

1139. Acra-Amman, Katrin. 'The Lady is in Jail.' *Monday Morning* 4–10 Nov., 1974, pp. 8–12.

1140. Afnan Shahid, Bahia. 'Women on the Warpath.' *Monday Morning* 9–15 July, 1973, pp. 4–10.

1141. Alouche, R. 'La femme libanaise et la travail.' *Travaux et Jours* 52 (July–Sept. 1974):61–70.

1142. Alouche, R. 'Image and Status of Women in the Lebanese Press.' (Text in French.) Research project in progress sponsored by the Institute for Women's Studies in the Arab World, Beirut University College, Beirut, Lebanon.

1143. Alouche, R. 'L'image de la femme à travers le roman libanais.' *Travaux et Jours* 47 (Apr.–June 1973): 73–90.

1144. Alouche, R. 'Roman et réalité sociale libanaise.' *Travaux et Jours* 45 (1972):83–93.

1145. D'Ancezune, H. Rostan. 'Sens religieux du mariage.' *Travaux et Jours* (Jan.–Feb. 1962):41–51.

1146. Awwad, Tawfiq Yusuf. *Death in Beirut*. Washington, D.C.: Three Continents Press, 1978.

1147. Bagros, Sylvie. 'Lorsqu'une française épouse un libanais: étude de cas.' *Travaux et Jours* 52 (July–Sept. 1974):39–60.

1148. Bayoudh, Edma. *A Study of 500 Cases of Women in Industry in Lebanon.* National Young Women's Christian Association, Beirut, Lebanon, 1968.

1149. Bayoudh, Edma and Ghorayyib, Rose. *Status of Women in Lebanon.* National Young Women's Christian Association, Beirut, Lebanon, 1951.

1150. Beirut University College. Alumnae Association. 'Laws Affecting Women in Lebanon.' Debate in Arabic held on 11 Feb., 1975 at Beirut University College. (English résumé and tape available at the Institute for Women's Studies in the Arab World Documentation Center.)

1151. Bushakra, Mary. *I Married an Arab.* New York: Day, 1951.

1152. Chamie, Mary. 'Sexuality and Birth Control Decisions among Lebanese Couples.' *Signs: Journal of Women in Culture and Society* 3, 1 (Autumn 1977): 294–312.

1153. Chamie, Marie and Harfouche, Jamal. 'Indigenous Midwives in Lebanon.' Final report submitted to the Smithsonian Institution Interdisciplinary Communication Program, 31 July, 1976.

1154. Chamoun, Mounir. 'Les femmes dans la société libanaise: couples.' *Travaux et Jours* 52 (July–Sept. 1974): 5–14. (Special Issue on Women in Lebanese Society.)

1155. Chamoun, Mounir. 'Image de la mère et sexualité au Liban.' *Travaux et Jours* 44 (July–Sept. 1972): 107–114.

1156. Chamoun, Mounir. 'Problèmes de la famille au Liban.' *Travaux et Jours* 25 (Oct.–Dec. 1967): 13–40.

1157. Charara, Yolla Polity. 'Femmes et politiques au Liban.' *Revue Française d'Etudes Politiques Méditerranéennes* no. 24 (1976): 65–76.

1158. Charara, Yolla Polity. *L'image de la femme dans la presse féminine au Liban: recherche effectué en 1971.* Beirut: Institut des Sciences Sociales, Université Libanaise, 1974.

1159. Charara, Yolla Polity. *La presse féminine au Liban.* Beyrouth: Imprimerie Catholique, 1970.

1160. Chehab, Leila. *Lebanese Women in the Fields of Education and Labour.* Embassy of Lebanon, Washington, D.C., 1975.

1161. Chidiac. M. 'Travail des femmes et des enfants.' *Mélanges Proche-Orientaux d'Economie Politique, Annales de la Faculté de Droit* (*Beyrouth*) (1965): 79–127.

1162. Deeb, Mary Jane A. 'The Khazin Family: a Case of the Effect of Social Change on Traditional Roles.' M.A. thesis, American University of Cairo, Egypt, Jan. 1972.

1163. Denneth, Charlotte. 'The Lebanese Woman and the Law—a Crusade to Abolish Man's Upper Hand Here.' *Daily Star*, 30 Dec., 1974, p. 7.

1164. Des Villettes, J. 'La vie des femmes dans un village maronite libanais, Ain el Kharoube.' *Revue de l'Institut des Belles Lettres Arabes* 23, 90 (1960): 151–207; 25, 91 (1961):271–279. (Also published Tunis, N. Bascone and S. Mucat, 1964.)

1165. 'An Examination of the Attitudes of Young Lebanese Women.' *Middle East Forum* 40 (June 1964):16 (original survey carried out in French by *l'Orient*, 21 May, 1964).

1166. Farsoun, Samih K. 'Family Structure in a Modernizing Society: Lebanon.' Ph.D. dissertation, University of Connecticut, 1971.

1167. Farsoun, Samih and Farsoun, K. 'Class and Patterns of Association among Kinsmen in Contemporary Lebanon.' *Anthropological Quarterly* 47 (1974): 93–111.

1168. 'Five Sectarian Juliets.' *Monday Morning*, 4–10 Nov., 1974, pp. 13–20.

1169. Fuller, Anne H. *Buarij: Portrait of a Lebanese Muslim Village.* Cambridge, Mass.: Harvard University Press, 1961.

1170. Germanos-Ghazaly, L. 'La femme et la terre.' *Travaux et Jours* no. 56–57 (July–Dec. 1975):75–94.

1171. Hamalian, Arpi. 'Armenian Women in Urban Occupations: a Cross-Cultural Analysis.' Paper presented at the Wellesley Conference on Women and

Development, Wellesley College, Mass., 2–6 June, 1976.

1172. Hamalian, Arpi. 'The Shirkets: Visiting Pattern of Armenians in Lebanon.' *Anthropological Quarterly* 47 (Jan. 1974):71–92.

1173. Hamdan, Hussein. 'The Lebanese Woman and National Development. Present Situation and Horizons of Progress.' Paper presented at the Conference on Arab Women in National Development, sponsored by UNICEF, Arab League and Arab States Adult Functional Literacy Center, Cairo, Egypt, 24–30 Sept., 1972.

1174. Harfouche, Jamal Karam. *Social Structure of Low-Income Families in Lebanon.* Beirut: Khayat, 1965.

1175. Hazou, Micheline. 'Petticoat Power.' *Monday Morning,* 8–14 Aug., 1977, pp. 26–27.

1176. Howell, D. 'Health Rituals at a Lebanese Shrine.' *Middle East Studies* 6 (1970):179–188.

1177. 'Institute for Women's Studies in the Arab World.' *WIN News* 3 (Winter 1977):60.

1178. Jabra, Nancy. 'The Role of Women in a Lebanese Community.' Ph.D. dissertation, Catholic University of America, Washington, D.C., 1975.

1179. Joly, Gertrude. 'The Women of the Lebanon.' *Royal Central Asian Society Journal* 38 (Apr.–July 1951): 177–184.

1180. Joseph, Suad. 'Counter Institutions or Institutions: the Role of Women in Community Formation in an Urban Lower Class Lebanese Neighborhood.' Paper presented at the Wellesley Conference on Women and Development, Wellesley College, Mass., 2–6 June, 1976.

1181. Joseph, Suad. 'Urban Poor Women in Lebanon: Does Poverty Have Public and Private Domains?' Paper presented at the 8th Annual Convention of the Association of the Arab-American University Graduates, Chicago, 17–19 Oct., 1975.

1182. Kallab, Ilham. 'Concept of Women in Children's Textbooks.' (Chiefly in Arabic). Research project sponsored by the Institute for Women's Studies in the Arab World, Beirut University College, Lebanon, 1979.

1183. Khal, Helen. 'A Study of the Works of Lebanese Women Artists (Accompanied by Slides).' Research project sponsored by the Institute for Women's Studies in the Arab World, Beirut University College, Lebanon, 1979.

1184. Khalaf, Samir. 'Family Associations in Lebanon.' *Journal of Comparative Family Studies* 2 (Autumn 1971):235–250.

1185. Khalaf, Samir. *Prostitution in a Changing Society: a Sociological Survey of Legal Prostitution in Beirut.* Beirut: Khayat, 1965.

1186. Khalaf, Samir and Kongstad, P. *Hamra of Beirut: a Case of Rapid Urbanization.* Leiden: E.J. Brill, 1973.

1187. Khuri, Fuad I. *From Village to Suburb: Order and Change in Greater Beirut.* Chicago: University of Chicago Press, 1975.

1188. Lahoud, Aline. 'In Search of the Lebanese Woman.' *Middle East Forum* 36 (1960):18–22.

1189. 'Laure Moghaizel: La liberation du corps social nécessite la libération des femmes.' *L'Orient–Le Jour*, 16 Oct., 1974.

1190. Mazas, P. 'La semaine sociale de Beyrouth: les droits de la femme.' *En Terre d'Islam* no. 23 (1948):109–114.

1191. Mirshak, Myra. 'Campaign to Elect "Ideal Mother" of Lebanon Organized by Committee.' *Daily Star*, 13 Mar., 1975.

1192. Mirshak, Myra. 'Divorce—Lebanese Style.' *Monday Morning*, 2–8 Apr., 1973, pp. 14–17.

1193. Mirshak, Myra. 'Lebanon's Unwed Mothers.' *Monday Morning*, 20–26 Aug., 1973, pp. 12–13.

1194. Moukaddem, Tuaam R. 'The Exercise of Lebanese Women of their Right to Vote.' Paper presented at the 17th Conference of the International Federation of University Women, Philadelphia, Aug. 1971.

1195. Mourani, H. and Chamoun, M. 'Controverse—image de la mère et sexualité au Liban.' *Travaux et Jours* 46 (Jan.–Mar., 1973):131–139.

1196. Najjar, S. 'The Status of Women in Lebanese Moslem Villages.' M.A. thesis, School of Arts and Sciences, American University of Beirut, 1967.

1197. Nallino, M. 'Discussione per la concessione alla donna libanesa della parità cogli uomini nel godimento dei diritti politici.' (Discussions about the Possibility of Giving Lebanese Women Equality of Political Rights with Men.) *Oriente Moderno* 31, 7–9 (1951): 132.

1198. Nuwayri, Jumana. 'Government in Skirts.' *Monday Morning* 14–20 Oct., 1974, pp. 9–12.

1199. Phares, Dr. Joseph, Di Napoli, George, S.J. and Lorfing, Irene. *A Survey of Rural Household Resource Allocation in Lebanon in 1975*. Beirut: Institute for Women's Studies in the Arab World and FAO, 1978.

1200. Prothro, Edwin Terry. *Child Rearing in the Lebanon*. Cambridge, Mass.: Harvard University Press, 1961.

1201. Sabri, Marie A. *Pioneering Profiles: Beirut College for Women*. Beirut: Khayat, 1967.

1202. Sayegh, Salma. 'Quelques aspects d'humanisme au Liban.' Présenté à l'occasion de la Troisième Session de la Commission des Droits de la Femme. Beyrouth, Mar. 1949. (Text in Arabic and French.)

1203. Sbaity, Fatima. 'Job Opportunities for American University of Beirut—Lebanese Women Graduates and their Impact on National Development.' Master's thesis, American University of Beirut, 1970.

1204. Shahid, Bahia Afnan. 'Women on the Warpath.' *Monday Morning*, 9–15 July, 1973, pp. 4–10.

1205. Sukkarieh, Bassimah Elias. 'Divorce Factors among the Greek Orthodox in Beirut.' M.A. thesis, School of Arts and Sciences, American University of Beirut, 1960.

1206. Sweet, L.E. 'Visiting Patterns and Social Dynamics in a Lebanese Druze Village.' *Anthropological Quarterly* 47 (1974): 112–119.

1207. Sweet, L.E. 'The Women of Ain ed Dayr.' *Anthropological Quarterly* 40, 3 (July 1967): 167–183.

1208. Tarcici, A. *L'éducation actuelle de la jeune fille musul-mane au Liban.* Vitry-sur-Seine: Librairie Mariale, 1941.
1209. Tawile, Maurice. 'La femme Libanaise au travail.' *Action Proche-Orient* 21 (1963):39–43.
1210. Tomeh, Aida K. *Birth Order and Alienation among College Women in Lebanon.* Ohio: Bowling Green State University, 1976.
1211. Touma, Toufic. *Un village de montagne au Liban (Hadeth el Jabbé).* Paris: Mouton, 1958.
1212. UNESCO. National Lebanese Commission. *Report on the Relationship between Educational Opportunities and Employment Opportunities for Women.* Paris: UNESCO, 1974. (Monograph on Lebanon published in French in 1973.)
1213. UNESCO. 'Report on the Relationship between Educational Opportunities and Employment Opportunities for Women—a Study of Five Countries (Argentina, Ivory Coast, Lebanon, Sierra Leone, Sri Lanka)' (ED–74/WS/56). Paris: UNESCO, 20 July, 1975.
1214. United Nations. Economic and Social Council. Economic Commission for Western Asia. 'Institutions and Organizations concerned with the Participation of Lebanese Rural Women in Development' (E/ECWA/SDHS/1), 23 Oct., 1974. (Revised Jan. 1977.)
1215. United Nations. World Health Organization. 'Family Formation Patterns and Health: an International Collaborative Study in India, Iran, Lebanon, Philippines and Turkey.' Geneva: WHO, 1976.
1216. Van Dusen, Roxann A. 'The Establishment of a Community Health Clinic: a Case Study in a Lebanese Suburb.' (Summary of Social Change and Decision-Making: Family Planning in Lebanon.) Doctoral dissertation, Johns Hopkins University, Baltimore, Md., 1973. Paper presented at the Meeting of American Association for the Advancement of Science, New York, 26–31 Jan., n.d.
1217. Van Dusen, Roxann A. 'Natives and Newcomers:

Women in a Suburb of Beirut, Lebanon.' Paper presented at the Wellesley Conference on Women and Development, Wellesley College, Mass., 2–6 June, 1976.

1218. Van Dusen, Roxann A. 'Social Networks Within an Arab Female Community on the Outskirts of Beirut.' Paper presented at the 7th Annual Middle East Studies Association Meeting, Milwaukee, Wis., Nov., 1973.

1219. Wigle, Laurel D. 'Economic and Political Activities of Village Women in Lebanon.' Paper presented at the Annual Meeting of the American Anthropological Association, Mexico City, Nov. 1974.

1220. Williams, Judith R. *The Youth of Haouch el-Harimi*. Cambridge, Mass.: Harvard University Press, 1968.

1221. 'Women and the Next Parliamentary Elections.' *Daily Star*, 8, 9, 10, 11 Aug., 1975.

1222. Women's International League for Peace and Freedom. *Report from the Lebanese Section on the Middle East, 1970*.

1223. Yammine, Randa. 'Do you Want a Woman to Rule You?' *Monday Morning* 17–21 Oct., 1974, pp. 20–22.

1224. Yankey, D. *Fertility Differences in a Modernizing Country: a Survey of Lebanese Couples*. Princeton: Princeton University Press, 1961.

1225. Zurayk, Huda C. 'The Effect of Education of Women and Urbanization on Actual and Desired Fertility Control in Lebanon.' *Population Bulletin of the United Nations Economic Commission for Western Asia* no. 13 (July 1977): 32–41.

LIBYA

1226. Abdel Kafi. *Les mariages en Tripolitaine*. Tripoli: Libyan Publishing House, 1964.

1227. Babbitt, A.E. 'Changes Come to Libya.' *UN Review* 4 (May 1958):18–20.

1228. Fikry, M. 'La femme et les conflits de valeurs en Libye.' *Revue de l'Occident Musulman et de la Méditerranée* no. 18 (1974): 93–110.

1229. Libya. Ministry of Education. 'Women Education in Libya.' Paper submitted by the Delegation of the Kingdom of Libya to the Conference of Ministers of Education and Ministers of Economic Planning in Arab States, Tripoli, 1966.

1230. 'Loi relative à la protection des droits de la femme à l'héritage en Libye.' *Cahiers de l'Orient Contemporain* 39 (1 Jan.–30 April 1959).

1231. Mason, John Paul. 'Sex and Symbol in the Treatment of Women: the Wedding Rite in a Libyan Oasis Community.' *American Ethnologist* 2, 4 (Nov. 1975):6490–6661. (Special Issue on Sex Roles in Cross-Cultural Perspectives.)

1232. Mead, Richard and George, Alan. 'The Women of Libya.' *Middle East International* no. 25 (July 1973): 18–20.

1233. Miladi, Khadija. 'Interview on the Status of Women in Libya.' *Women International Network News* 3, 2 (1977):60.

1234. Nijim, Basheer, *Sex Ratio and Landholding Patterns in Libya.* Iowa: University of Northern Iowa, 1975.

1235. Souriau, C. 'La société féminine en Libye.' *Revue de l'Occident Musulman et de la Méditerranée* 6 (le et 2ème trimestre 1969):127–155.

MAURITANIA

1236. ILO. Office of Public Information. 'Mauritania: Women Weave their Future—an ILO Project for the Development of Rug Weaving, Wool Produc-

tion and Management.' *Management and Productivity* 2, 33 (1970).
1237. *Mariémou. Revue du Mouvement National des Femmes du Parti du Peuple Mauritanien*, 1969– , quarterly. (French and Arabic texts.) Nouakchott, Mauritania.

MOROCCO

1238. Al-Amin, A. 'L'évolution de la femme et le problème du mariage au Maroc.' *Présence Africaine* (Revue de l'Institut de Sociologie), (4ème trim. 1968):32–51.
1239. Attia, A. 'Colloque international sur les relations d'autorité dans la famille maghrébine.' *Revue de l'Institut des Belles Lettres Arabes* (1967):303–308.
1240. Baron, A.M. 'La femme dans le prolétariat marocain.' *Masses Ouvrières* no. 118 (1956):84–91.
1241. Bastide, Henri de la. 'Une grande famille du sud Marocain: Les Ma el-Ainin.' *Maghréb-Machrék-Monde Arabe* no. 56 (Mar.–Apr. 1973):37–39.
1242. Belghiti, Malika. 'Les relations féminines et le statut de la femme dans la famille rurale.' *Bulletin Economique et Social du Maroc* 31 (1969):1–74. (Also in *Etudes Sociologiques sur le Maroc* (1971):289–361.)
1243. Belghiti, Malika. 'Le statut de la femme dans trois villages de la Tessaout (Maroc).' *Lamalif* 45 (Jan.–Feb. 1971):28–31.
1244. Belghiti, Malika, Chraibi, Najat and Tamou, A. 'La ségrégation des garçons et des filles à la campagne.' *Bulletin Economique et Social du Maroc* 33, 120–121 (1971):81–144.
1245. Ben-Ami, Issachar. 'Le mariage traditionnel chez les juifs marocains.' *Folklore Research Center Studies* 4 (1974):9–103.
1246. Benhadji Serradj, M. 'Quelques usages féminins populaires à Tlemcen (contribution à l'étude du

folklore maghrébin).' *Revue de l'Institut des Belles Lettres Arabes* 14 (1951): 279–292.

1247. Bennani, Mesdal. 'Quelques considérations sur la prostitution au Maroc.' *Revue Tunisienne des Sciences Sociales* 4, 11 (1967): 79–84.

1248. Berhnheim, N. 'Révolution féminine au Maghreb.' *Jeune Afrique* no. 549 (15 June, 1971): 55–59.

1249. Bolo, Etienne. 'Les adolescents maghrébins des cités de transit.' *Peuples Méditerranéens* no. 2 (Jan.–Mar. 1978): 97–118.

1250. Borrmans, Maurice. *Statut personnel et famille au Maghreb de 1940 à nos jours.* The Hague: Mouton, 1977.

1251. Bousser, M. and Khellad, A. 'Enquête sur le trousseau et le sdaq au Maroc.' *Afrique* (le et 2e trimestre 1942): 102–155.

1252. Brom, Kenneth. *People of Sali: Tradition and Change in a Moroccan City 1830–1930.* Cambridge, Mass.: Harvard University Press, 1976.

1253. Buttin, P. 'Ombres et lumières sur le Maroc: la promotion féminine.' *Confluent* (1962): 466–475.

1254. Cazautets, J. 'Les mariages consanguins dans la plaine du Loukkos.' *Revue de Géographie du Maroc* 8 (1965): 35–40.

1255. Celarié, Henriette. *Behind Moroccan Walls.* Plainview, New York: Books for Libraries, 1970.

1256. Centre d'Etudes et de Recherches Démographiques. *La fécondite marocaine.* Rabat: Direction de la Statistique, 1974.

1257. Centre d'Etudes et de Recherches Démographiques. *La nuptualité.* Rabat: Direction de la Statistique, 1975.

1258. Charnay, Jean-Paul. 'De la grande maison au couple moderne: Interférences entre droit, psychologie et économie dans l'évolution de la famille maghrébine.' *Revue Algérienne des Sciences Juridiques, Economiques et Politiques* 11, 3 (1974): 57–83.

1259. 'Colloque maghrébin de la femme rurale.' *L'Action,* 6 Apr., 1968.

1260. 'Colloque sur les problèmes de l'émancipation de la

femme marocaine.' *Al-Kifah al-Watani* 18–19 June, 1967, pp. 18–22.

1261. Daoud, Z. al Achgar, and Chkounda, H. 'Les mariages mixtes (Maroc).' *Revue de Presse* no. 109 (1966).

1262. Davis, Susan. *The Determinants of Social Position Among Rural Moroccan Women.* Trenton, N.J., 1975.

1263. Davis, Susan. 'Liberated Women in a Moroccan Village: the Wages of Self Support.' Paper presented at the 8th Annual Middle East Studies Association Meeting, Boston, 6–9 Nov., 1974.

1264. Davis, Susan. 'A Separate Reality: Moroccan Village Women.' Paper presented at the 7th Annual Middle East Studies Association Meeting, Milwaukee, Wis., 8–10 Nov., 1973.

1265. Decrop, M. 'Comment concevoir l'éducation sexuelle chez les musulmans marocains.' *Maroc-Médical* 306 (1950): 1058–1060.

1266. Decroux, Paul. 'Le problème du status personnel au Maroc.' *Travaux et Jours* 4 (Jan.–Feb. 1962): 69–80.

1267. Deprez, J. 'Mariage mixte, Islam et nation (à propos d'une récente campagne contre mariage mixte des marocains).' *Revue Algérienne* 12 (1975): 97–142.

1268. Duchac, J. *et al.* 'Villes et sociétés au Maghreb: études sur l'urbanisation.' *Middle East Journal* 31, 2 (1977): 220–1.

1269. Dughi, N. and Patron, M. 'Daughter of the Sultan.' *Ladies Home Journal* 74 (Dec. 1957): 52–53.

1270. Dwyer, D.H. *Images and Self-Images.* New York: Columbia University Press, 1978.

1271. Dwyer, D.H. 'The Impact of Women on Religion in a Moroccan Village.' Paper presented at the 72nd Annual Meeting of the American Anthropological Association, New Orleans, La., 28 Nov.–2 Dec., 1973.

1272. Dwyer, D.H. 'Moroccan Woman in a Traditional Urban Setting: an Analysis of their Conflict Behaviors.' Ph.D. dissertation, Yale University, 1973.

1273. Dwyer, D.H. 'Moroccan Woman, Cultural Concepts about her Development.' Paper presented at the 7th

E

Annual Middle East Studies Association Meeting, Milwaukee, Wis., 8–10 Nov., 1973.

1274. Dwyer, D.H. 'Sexual Ideology and Systems of Partial Consciousness: the Moroccan Case.' Paper presented at the 75th Annual Meeting of the American Anthropological Association, Washington, D.C., 17–21 Nov., 1976.

1275. 'Eduquer la femme, c'est éduquer la nation.' *L'Opinion,* 12 Aug., 1971.

1276. Eickelman, Dale F. *Moroccan Islam: Tradition and Society in a Pilgrimate Center.* Austin: University of Texas Press, 1976.

1277. El-Fasi, Mohammad. *Chants anciens des femmes de Fès.* Paris: Seghers, 1967.

1278. 'La femme marocaine.' *Révolution Africaine,* Nov. 1966, pp. 8–13.

1279. Fernea, Elizabeth. *A Street in Marrakesh: a Personal Encounter with the Lives of Moroccan Women.* New York: Doubleday, 1975.

1280. Forget, Nelly. 'Attitudes towards Work by Women in Morocco.' *International Social Science Journal* 14, 1 (1962):92–124.

1281. Francisi, A. 'Marocco: l'emancipazione della donna in una intervista della principessa "Aisha".' (An Interview with Princess Aisha of Morocco on the Emancipation of Women.) *Oriente Moderno* 45, 7–9 (1965):777.

1282. Gentric, H. *La promotion de la femme au Maghreb: recherches bibliographiques depuis 1950.* Paris: Institut National des Techniques de la Documentation, 1967.

1283. Goichon, A.M. 'La femme de la moyenne bourgeoisie Fasiya.' *Revue des Etudes Islamiques* 3 (1929):1–74.

1284. Graff-Wassink, M.W. 'Opinion Survey on Mixed Marriages in Morocco.' *Journal of Marriage and the Family* 29 (1967):527–589.

1285. Hassar, F. 'L'émancipation de la femme marocaine.' *Confluent* 21 (1958):210–213.

1286. Al-Hassar, M. 'The Special Problems of Young Women and Mothers with Regard to their Families and

Professional Careers.' Paper presented at the International Conference of Parents Associations, Ministry of Education, Morocco, 22–28 July, 1962.

1287. El-Hassar-Zeghari, Latifa. 'La femme marocaine et sa préparation à la vie familiale et professionnelle.' *Confluent* no. 23–24 (Sept.–Oct. 1962):641–668.

1288. Hoffman, Bernard G. *The Structure of Traditional Moroccan Rural Society*. The Hague: Mouton, 1967.

1289. Jacobs, Milton. 'The Moroccan Jewess: a Study in Cultural Stability and Change.' Ph.D. dissertation, Catholic University of America, 1957.

1290. El-Jazouli, N. 'Les causes de l'instabilité du mariage, les modes de dissolution du marriage en droit marocain.' *Revue Algérienne des Sciences Juridiques, Economiques et Politiques* 4, 4 (1968):1117–1126.

1291. Lahlou, Abbes. 'Etudes sur la famille traditionnelle de Fès.' *Revue de l'Institut de Sociologie* no. 3 (1968): 407–441.

1292. Lahlou, Abbes. 'Etudes sur la famille traditionnelle au Maroc: le mariage à Fés.' *Revue de l'Institut des Belles Lettres Arabes* 33, 26 (1970):323–64.

1293. Lallement, Anne-Marie. 'Le colloque, la femme et la féminité dans le Maghreb et la plateforme du groupe "Femmes Algériennes".' *Peuples Méditerranéens* 5 (Oct.–Dec. 1978):147–150.

1294. Lapham, Robert J. 'Family Planning, Attitudes and Knowledge among Married Women in Central Morocco.' Paper presented at the Annual Meeting of the Population Association of America, Boston, 1968.

1295. Lapham, Robert J. 'L'utilisation passée ou présente de la contraception chez les femmes du milieu urbain et rurale dans la plaine des Sais du Maroc.' *Revue Tunisienne de Sciences Sociales* 6, 17–18 (1969): 439–455.

1296. Lecomte, Jean and Montagne, Joel. *Maternal and Child Health and Family Planning in Morocco: a Preliminary Bibliography*, No. 7. North Carolina: University of North Carolina, 1974.

1297. Maher, Vanessa. 'Divorce and Property in the Middle Atlas of Morocco.' *Man* 9, 1 (1974):103–22.
1298. Maher, Vanessa. 'Social Stratification and the Role of Women in the Middle Atlas of Morocco.' Ph.D. dissertation, University of Cambridge, 1972.
1299. Maher, Vanessa. *Women and Property in Morocco: Their Changing Relation to the Process of Social Stratification in the Middle Atlas.* London: Cambridge University Press, 1975.
1300. Malka, Elie. *Essai sur la condition juridique de la femme juive au Maroc.* Paris: Librairie Générale de Droit et Jurisprudence, 1952.
1301. Martenson, Mona. 'Attitudes vis-à-vis du travail professionel de la femme marocaine: une enquête preliminaire.' *Bulletin Economique et Social du Maroc* 28, 100 (1966):133–146.
1302. Mendo, C.R. *Antropologia de la mujer marroqui musulmana.* Tetuan: Editorial Marroqui, 1953.
1303. Mernissi, Fatima. 'Avoir et sexe dans un bureaucratie moderne: la relation entre personnel paramédical et les usagers illétres du service de santé publique comme un champ de lutte de classes.' Paper contributed to a special issue of the North African Directory, 1977. (Mimeographed.)
1304. Mernissi, Fatima. *Beyond the Veil: Male–Female Dynamics in a Modern Muslim State.* New York: Halsted Press, 1975. (Résumé available in *WIN News* 3, 1 (Winter 1977):63–65.)
1305. Mernissi, Fatima. 'Dim Prospects of Women's Liberation through Work in a Developing Economy: the Characteristics of the Average Moroccan Female Worker.' Paper presented at the Debate Week on Women held at the Institute of Ethnology and Anthropology, Copenhagen University, 10–14 Mar., 1975.
1306. Marnissi, Fatima. 'The Impact of Sexual Ideology on Labor Market in Moslem Morocco.' Paper presented to the Research Committee on Sex Roles at the 8th Congress of International Sociology, 19–23 Aug., 1974.

1307. Mernissi, Fatima. 'Male–Female Dynamics in a Moslem Society: Morocco.' Ph.D. dissertation, Brandeis University, Mass., 1973.
1308. Mernissi, Fatima. 'Women's Solidarity in the Courtyards of Saints' Tombs: Morocco.' Paper presented at the Wellesley Conference on Women and Development, Wellesley College, Mass., 2–6 June, 1976.
1309. Molinari. *L'évolution de la femme marocaine.* Paris: Centre de Hautes Etudes d'Administration Musulmane, 1958.
1310. 'Morocco.' *WIN News* 2 (Summer 1976):35.
1311. 'Morocco "Berber Country Women".' *Guardian* (London), May 1976. (Also in *WIN News* 2, 3 (1976):35.)
1312. Morris, Constance Lily. *Behind Moroccan Walls.* New York: Books for Libraries Press, 1970.
1313. Morsey, Magaly. 'La femme et la politique au Maroc.' *Revue Française d'Etudes Politiques Méditerranéennes* no. 24 (1976):77–86.
1314. 'Moslem World: Beyond the Veil.' *Time*, 11 Nov., 1957, pp. 32–36.
1315. Nouacer, Khadija. 'The Changing Status of Women and the Employment of Women in Morocco.' *International Social Science Journal* 14 (1962): 124–129.
1316. Nouacer, Khadija. 'Femmes et professions au Maroc. Evolution et travail de la femme au Maroc.' *Revue Internationale des Sciences Sociales* 16, 1 (1962): 124–130.
1317. 'Opinions de marocains sur les problèmes de la famille et de la promotion de la femme.' *Documents Nord-Africains* (Sept. 1965).
1318. 'Pour la promotion de la femme marocaine.' *Maroc-Documents* 6 (1969):69–89.
1319. 'La promotion féminine.' *Maroc* 7 (1966):29–37.
1320. Rassam, Amal (Vinogradov, Amal Rassam). 'French Colonialism as Reflected in the Male-Female Interaction in Morocco.' *Transactions of the New York Academy of Sciences* 36, 2 (1974):192–199.
1321. Rassam, Amal (Vinogradov, Amal Rassam). 'Trans-

formation of Women's Roles in Rural Morocco.' Research project in progress at the Department of Anthropology, Queens College, City University of New York, Flushing, New York.

1322. Rassam, Amal (Vinogradov, Amal Rassam). 'Women and Power: the Politics of Domestic Interaction in Morocco.' Anthropology Department, Queens College, City University of New York, n.d.

1323. Schaefer, Davis Susan. 'Terminological Problems in the Anthropological Study of Women (Morocco).' New Jersey, Trenton State College, 1975.

1324. Selosse, J. 'Tradition et modernisme, perception de changement social par une population citadine marocaine.' *Revue Française de Sociologie* 4, 2 (Apr.–June 1963):144–158.

1325. 'Some Slave Girls of Morocco.' *Muslim World* 26 (1936):176–185.

1326. 'Soucis et souvenirs de trois jeunes femmes marocaines.' (Interview.) *Confluent* no. 11 (Jan.–Feb. 1961): 17–19.

1327. Tobi, Anessa. 'La condition de la femme marocaine.' *Vie Sociale* 7–8 (1973):390–398.

1328. Uplegger, H. 'Djellaba und Litham: zur Verschleierung der arabischen Frau in Marokko.' *Bustan* 9, 2 (1968):22–26.

1329. Vaucher-Zananiri, N. 'L'émancipation de la femme au Maghreb.' *Preuves-Informations* (1964):405.

1330. 'Veiled Morocco.' *Vogue* 158, Dec. 1971, pp. 116–123.

1331. Vinogradov, Amal Rassam. 'The Ait Ndhir of Morocco: a Study of the Social Transformation of a Berber Tribe.' Anthropological Papers, no. 55. Ann Arbor, Mich., 1974.

1332. Vinogradov, Amal Rassam. 'Cultural Values, Economic Realities and Rural Women in Morocco: Contradictions and Accommodations.' Paper presented at the Wellesley Conference on Women and Development, Wellesley College, Mass., 2–6 June, 1976.

1333. Westermarck, Edward. *Marriage Ceremonies in Morocco*. London: Macmillan, 1914.

1334. 'Women.' *Time*, 23 Jan., 1956, p. 26.
1335. El Yacoubi, R. 'La femme et son rôle déterminant dans la réussite du planning familial.' Mémoire de licence sciences économiques, Faculté des Sciences Juridiques, Economiques et Sociales, Mohammad V University, Rabat, 1972–1973.
1336. Zagouri, A. 'Les reprises de la femme après la dissolution de l'union conjugale célébrée "more judaico".' *Revue Marocaine de Droit* 17 (1965):1–4.
1337. El-Zeghari, Hassan. 'La femme marocaine et sa participation à la vie familiale et professionelle.' *Confluent* 23–24 (Sept.–Oct. 1962).

OMAN

1338. Heard-Bey, F. 'Social Changes in the Gulf States and Oman.' *Asian Affairs* 59 (Part 3, 1972):309–15.
1339. Mercer, Dennis. 'In the Arabian Gulf: Interview with Fatima Ahmed of the Omani Women's Movement.' *Liberation Support Movement News* 2 (Fall 1975).
1340. UNICEF. 'A New Dawn for Oman and its Women: Third World Women.' *UNICEF News* 76 (1973): 26–30.
1341. Wikan, Unni. 'Man Becomes Woman: Transsexualism in Oman as a Key to Gender Roles.' *Man* 12 (Aug. 1977):304–319.

PALESTINE

1342. Abu Daleb, Nuha. 'Palestinian women and their role in the revolution.' *Peuples Méditerranéens* no. 5 (Oct.–Dec. 1978):35–47.

1343. El-Aref, Aref. *Bedouin Love, Law and Legend, Dealing Exclusively with the Badu of Beersheba.* New York: AMS Press, 1974. (Reprint of the 1944 edition.)

1344. Barzilai, S. and Davies, A.M. 'Personality and Social Aspects of Mental Disease in Jerusalem Women.' *International Journal of Social Psychology* 18 (1972):22–28.

1345. Canaan, T. 'Unwritten Laws affecting the Arab Woman of Palestine.' *Journal of Palestine Oriental Society* 11 (1931):172–203.

1346. 'Celebrating International Women's Day. Woman: the Struggle for Liberation.' (Includes Women of Palestine.) *Guardian,* March 1977. (Supplement. From 33 West 17th St., New York, N.Y. 10011.)

1347. Fedorova, Zinaida. 'Our Hosts the Palestinian Women.' *Women of the Whole World* no. 3 (1973):20–23.

1348. Fitch, Florence. *The Daughter of Abd Salam: the Story of a Peasant Woman of Palestine.* Boston: Badger, 1930.

1349. General Union of Palestine Women (1965–1974). 'Report on the Activities of the General Union of Palestinian Women.' Paper presented at the 2nd Conference of the General Union, Beirut, 5–10 Aug., 1974.

1350. Granqvist, Hilma. *Birth and Childhood among the Arabs: Studies in a Mohammedan Village in Palestine.* New York: AMS Press, 1975 (reprint of the 1947 edition).

1351. Granqvist, Hilma. *Marriage Conditions in a Palestine Village,* 2 Vols. Helsingfors: Akademische Buchhandlung, 1931–1935. (Reprinted in New York: AMS Press, 1975.)

1352. Jafarey, S.A. *et al.* 'Use of Medical, Para-Medical Personnel and Traditional Midwives in the Palestine Family Planning Program.' *Demography* 5 (1968): 646–679.

1353. El-Karmy, Nada. 'Democratic Popular Front for the Liberation of Palestine Women.' *Palestine Resistance Bulletin* 11 (Oct. 1971).

1354. 'Laila Khaled Answers some Questions.' *Risk* 7, 1 (1971).

1355. Mansour, Sylvie. 'Identity among Palestinian Youth: Male and Female Differentials.' *Journal of Palestine Studies* 6, 4 (Summer 1977):71–89. (Article derived from a Ph.D. dissertation presented to the University of Paris.)

1356. Marx, E.E. 'The Division of Domestic Tasks between Spouses among the Negev Bedouins.' Tel Aviv, 1966.

1357. Mogannam, Matiel. *Arab Women and the Palestine Problem*. Conn.: Hyperion Press, 1975.

1358. *The Palestinian Arab Women League, 1960–1965*. Beirut: Ras Beirut Press, 1965.

1359. 'Palestinian Women in Kuwait.' Paper presented at the 2nd Conference of the General Union of Palestinian Women, Kuwait, 5–10 Aug., 1974.

1360. Sebban-Khan, A. 'Le mariage arabo-musulman (Sūr-Baher, Jérusalem-Est).' *Folklore Research Center Studies* 4 (1974):141–166.

1361. Tawil, Ramonda. 'Return and Reminiscence of a Palestinian Woman.' *New Outlook* 15 (Nov.–Dec. 1971):29–35.

1362. *The Struggle of Palestinian Women*. Beirut: Palestine Research Center, 1975.

1363. Weir, S. and Kawar, Widad. 'Costumes and Wedding Customs in Bayt Dajan.' *Palestine Exploration Quarterly* 107 (1975):39–52.

1364. 'Women of Palestine: International Women's Year, 1975.' *American Near East Refugee Aid Newsletter* (ANERA) no. 33 (May–June 1975).

1365. Zu'bi, E. 'The Changing Status of Arab Women in Israel.' *Kidma* 2 (1975):31–33.

SAUDI ARABIA

1366. Alireza, Marianne. *At the Drop of a Veil*. Boston: Houghton Mifflin, 1971.

1367. Badran, Hoda. 'Report on the Mission to Saudi Arabia, 18 Oct.–17 Nov., 1975.' UNICEF and UNDP.

1368. Clifford, Mary Louise. *The Land and the People of the Arabian Peninsula*. New York: J.B. Lippincott, 1977.

1369. Cole, Donald. 'Social and Economic Structure of the Al Murrah: a Saudi Arabian Bedouin Tribe.' Ph.D. dissertation, University of California, Berkeley, 1971.

1370. Dearden, Ann, ed. *Arab Women*. Minority Rights Group Report, no. 27. London: Minority Rights Group, 1977. (From 36 Craven Street, London W.C.2.)

1371. 'Education of Women in Saudi Arabia.' *Muslim World* 46 (1956): 366–367.

1372. 'From a Correspondent in Jeddah . . . Restrictions Against Western Women.' *WIN News* 4, 3 (Summer 1978): 41.

1373. Hopwood, D. *The Arabian Peninsula: Society and Politics*. London: Allen and Unwin, 1972.

1374. Katakura, Motoko. *Bedouin Village: a Study of a Saudi Arabian People in Transition*. Tokyo: University of Tokyo Press, 1977.

1375. Musil, Alois. *The Manners and Customs of the Rwala Bedouins*. New York: AMS Press, 1977. (Reprint of the 1928 edn.)

1376. 'Public Execution of Saudi Princess and Husband.' *WIN News* 4, 2 (Spring 1978): 9.

1377. Reintjens, Hortense. *Die soziale Stellung der Frau bei den nordarabischen Beduinen unter besonderer Berücksichtigung ihrer Ehe-und Familienverhältnisse*. Bonn: Selbstverlag des Orientalischen Seminars der Universität, 1975.

1378. Sa'ad, N.M. 'Centre for Training and Applied Research in Community Development, Diriyah-Riyadh, Saudi Arabia.' Report of the Expert in Social Development (Women's Activities).

1379. 'Saudi Arabia—Escort Enigma.' *Sketch* (3 Aug., 1973): 46.

1380. Saudi Arabia. Permanent Mission to the UN. *The Modern Saudi Arabian Women*. Report of the Mission at the Conference of International Women's Year, Mexico City, 1975.

1381. Shammout, A. 'On Being a Sheik's Wife.' *Saturday Review* 50 (14 Oct., 1967): 71–72, 90–92.

1382. Thompson, D. 'Out of this World.' (Saudi Arabia.) *Ladies Home Journal* 69 (Aug. 1952): 11.

1383. Al-Torki, Soraya. 'Religion and Social Organization of Elite Families in Urban Saudi Arabia.' Ph.D. dissertation, University of California, Berkeley, 1973.

1384. Traini, R. 'Arabia Saudiana: associazione per l'elevazione della donna. La prima donna giornalista saudiana.' (Saudi Arabian Association for the Advancement of Women. The First Woman Journalist in Saudi Arabia.) *Oriente Moderno* 43, 6–7 (1963): 492–493.

1385. Traini, R. 'Arabia Saudiana: circa la libertà della donna nella scelta del marito.' (Polemics in Saudi Arabia on the Liberty of Women in the Choice of a Husband.) *Oriente Moderno* 44, 8–9 (1964): 588–589.

1386. Traini, R. 'Arabia Saudiana: richiamo dell'università islamica di Medina all'osservanza dell'uso del velo.' (The Islamic University of Medina Calls all Muslim Men to Oblige their Wives to Wear a Veil.) *Oriente Moderno* 42, 5 (1962): 460–461.

1387. Uzayzir, Z. and Chelhod, J. 'L'amour et le mariage dans le desert.' *Objets et Mondes*, 9 (1969): 269–278.

1388. 'Women and Travel: Saudi Arabia.' *WIN News* 3 (Autumn 1977): 63.

1389. Yassin, Anas Ibn Youssef. 'Behind that Veil.' Address presented to the Arab-American Women's Friendship Association, New York Church Center for the UN, 3 Mar., 1967.

SOMALIA

1390. Haji Elmi, Marian. 'Statement of the Leader of the Delegation of the Somali Democratic Republic in Mexico, International Women's Year, 1975.' *WIN News* 1, 4 (Oct. 1975):64.
1391. Hosken, Franziska P. 'Female Mutilation in Somalia Tests "Human Rights Doctrine".' *Politics and Other Human Interests* Issue 14 (9 May 1978): 21–22.
1392. 'Human Rights Violation in Somalia.' *WIN News* 4, 2 (Spring 1978):6–8.
1393. Lewis, I.M. *Marriage and the Family in Northern Somalia.* East African Studies Series, No. 15. Kampala: East African Institute of Social Research, 1962.
1394. Villeneuve, Anne de. 'Etude sur une coutume somalie: les femmes cousues.' *Journal de la Société des Africanistes* 6 (1937):15–32.

SUDAN

1395. Abdel-Mahmoud, Fatima. 'The Role of Sudanese Woman in Integrated Rural Development.' *WIN News* 1, 3 (June 1976):24.
1396. Abdel-Mahmoud, Fatima. 'The Status of Women in the Democratic Republic of Sudan.' Paper presented at the Seminar on the Role of Women in Integrated Rural Development with Emphasis on Population Problems, Cairo, Egypt, 26 Oct.–3 Nov., 1974.
1397. Akolawin, N. 'Personal Law in the Sudan: Trends and Developments.' *Journal of African Law* 17, 2 (1973): 149–195.

1398. Bannaga, Ali Mohayad. 'The Sudan—a Case Study.' Paper presented at the Seminar on the Role of Women in Integrated Rural Development with Emphasis on Population Problems, Cairo, Egypt, 26 Oct.–3 Nov., 1974.

1399. Bayoumi, Ahmed. 'The Training and Activity of Village Midwives in the Sudan.' *Tropical Doctor* 6, 3 (July 1976):118–125. (Résumé available in *WIN News* 3, 1 (Winter 1977):24.)

1400. Calame-Griaule, G. 'Le rôle spirituel et social de la femme dans la société soudanaise traditionnelle.' *Diogene* (Paris) no. 37 (1962):81–92.

1401. Clark, Isobel and Diaz, Christina. 'A Slow Change in Attitudes.' *WIN News* 4, 3 (Summer 1978):25–26.

1402. Cunnison, Ian. *The Baggara Arabs: Power and Lineage in a Sudanese Nomad Tribe.* Oxford, Clarendon Press, 1966.

1403. 'Excerpts from Studies by Dr. Fatima Abdel Mahmoud, Minister for Social Welfare in the Sudan.' *WIN News* 2 (Summer 1976):33.

1404. Farran, C. d'Olivier. *Matrimonial Laws of the Sudan.* Butterworth's African Law Series no. 7. London: Butterworth, 1963.

1405. Fawzi, S. 'The Rôle of Women in a Developing Sudan.' *Proceedings of the Institute of Differing Civilizations.* Brussels, 1958.

1406. Fluehr-Lobban, Carolyn. 'Women and Social Liberation. The Sudan Experience.' Arab-American University Graduates Information Papers no. 12, Mar. 1974.

1407. Fluehr-Lobban, Carolyn. 'Women in the Political Arena in the Sudan.' Paper presented at the 7th Annual Middle East Studies Association Meeting, Milwaukee, Wis., 8–10 Nov., 1973.

1408. Fluehr-Lobban, Carolyn. 'Women in Radical Political Movements in the Sudan.' Paper presented at the Wellesley Conference on Women and Development, Wellesley College, Mass., 2–6 June, 1976.

1409. Fluehr-Lobban, Carolyn. 'Women, the Law and Socio-Political Change in Sudan. University Myths about

Arab Women.' Paper presented at the 7th Annual Middle East Studies Association Meeting, Milwaukee, Wis., 8–10 Nov., 1973.

1410. Fluehr-Lobban, Carolyn. 'The Women's Movement in Sudan: its Place Among Arab Women's Struggles for National Liberation and Social Emancipation.' Paper presented at the 8th Annual Middle East Studies Association Meeting, Boston, 6–9 Nov., 1974.

1411. Francisi, A. 'Sudan: le donne e le elezioni.' (Women and Elections in the Sudan.) *Oriente Moderno* 45, 3 (1965):193–194.

1412. Gifoun, N. *et al.* 'A Woman's Place?' *Sudanow* 2, 11 (Nov. 1977):26–32.

1413. Giuliani, V. 'Sudan: proposta di legge sulla parificazione dei salari delle donne.' (A Draft Bill on the Equality of Salary for Men and Women in the Sudan.) *Oriente Moderno* 45 (1965):967–968.

1414. Hayes, Rose Oldfield. 'Female Genital Mutilation, Fertility Control, Women's Roles and the Patrilineage in Modern Sudan: a Functional Analysis.' *American Anthropologist* 2, 4 (Nov. 1975).

1415. Henin, R.A. 'Marriage Patterns and Trends in the Nomadic and Settled Populations of the Sudan.' *Africa* 39 (1969):238–259.

1416. 'Higher Education and Employment: Sudan, Tanzania and Zambia.' *Women at Work* (ILO) no. 3 (1971): 9–10.

1417. Hofmann, I. 'Heiratsbrüche im Gebiet von Alt-Dongola, Soudan.' (Marriage Customs in the Region of Upper Dongola, Sudan.) *Anthropos* (Fribourg) 67, 1–2 (1972):152–160.

1418. Ibrahim, Laila. 'Annual Report of Women's Employment Department.' Sudan: Ministry of Labour, 1971.

1419. Kendall, E.M. 'A Short History of the Training of Midwives in the Sudan.' *Sudan Notes and Records* 33, 7 (June 1952):42–53.

1420. Khayreya, Anwar. 'The Women in Al Hamam in the Western Desert.' Thesis for the Diploma at the

Institute of Social Sciences, University of Alexandria, 1969.

1421. Mahmoud, Fatma B. 'The Role of the Sudanese Women's Union in Sudanese Politics.' B.A. thesis, University of Khartoum, 1971.

1422. Richards, G.E. 'Adult Education Amongst Country Women: an Experiment at Umm Gerr.' *Sudan Notes and Records* 29, 2 (1948):225–227.

1423. 'The Role of Sudanese Women in Social Development.' Paper presented at the Regional Conference on Education, Vocational Training and Employment Opportunities for Girls and Women in African Countries, Rabat, Morocco, 2–29 May, 1971. *WIN News*, 2, 3 (1976):33.

1424. Saad, Mahasin. 'Notes on Higher Education for Women in the Sudan.' *Sudan Notes and Records* 53 (1972): 174–81.

1425. Sanderson, Lilian. 'Careers for Women in the Sudan Today.' *African Women* (June 1963):25–29.

1426. Sanderson, Lilian. 'Some Aspects of Development of Girls' Education in Northern Sudan.' *Sudan Notes and Records* 42 (1961):91–101.

1427. Sanderson, Lilian. 'University Education for Sudanese Women in African Perspectives.' *Sudan Society* no. 3 (1975):21–30.

1428. Shandall, A. Abdel Futuh. 'Circumcision and Infibulation of Females. A General Consideration of the Problem and a Clinical Study of the Complications in Sudanese Women.' *Sudan Medical Journal* 5 (1967):178.

1429. Sheik-ul-Din, Dina. 'How Sudanese Fare with Customary and State Law.' Paper presented at the Wellesley Conference on Women and Development, Wellesley College, Mass., 2–6 June, 1976.

1430. Smith, Margaret. 'The Sudanese Woman and her Outlook on Life.' *Muslim World* 14 (1924):143–147.

1431. Spelman, N.G. 'Women's Work in the Gezira, Sudan.' *Overseas Education* 26 (1954):66–69.

1432. 'Sudan: Interview with Dr. Asma el Darier, Medical

Officer at the Faculty of Medicine, University of Khartoum.' *WIN News* 4 (Winter 1978):51.

1433. Sudan. Ministry of Education. *Girls Education in the Sudan.* Educational Planning Unit Documentary Series no. 7. Khartoum: Publications Bureau, 1970.

1434. 'Sudan: Participation of the Ministry of Social Welfare in the Field of Women's Affairs.' *WIN News* 3 (Spring 1977):43.

1435. 'Sudan's Donkey—Black Midwives.' *Today's Health* (Jan. 1968):16–18.

1436. 'The Sudan Women's Union.' *WIN News* 3, 2 (Spring 1977):44.

1437. Suliman, Salma M. 'Women in Sudan Public Service.' *Sudan Journal of Administration and Development* 11 (Jan. 1966):37.

1438. 'The Third Congress of the Sudan Women's Union, April 20–24, 1976.' *WIN News* 2 (Autumn 1976): 53–54.

1439. Tubiana, J. 'Exogamie clanique et l'Islam: l'exemple Kobé—implications économiques et politiques du renoncement à l'exogamie en faveur du mariage avec la fille de l'oncle paternel.' *L'Homme* 15, 3–4 (1975):67–81.

1440. United Nations. Economic and Social Council. Economic Commission for Africa. Women's Programme in Collaboration with the Ministry of Health and Social Welfare, Sudan. 'Employment of Women in the Sudan' (M75–1335). Paper contributed to the ILO Comprehensive Employment Mission, Sudan, Jan. 1975.

1441. Volpi, B. 'Sudan: preparazione di una organizzazione femminile sudanese.' (Preparation of a Sudanese Feminist Organization.) *Oriente Moderno* 42, 10–11 (1962):878.

1442. Weil, Barbara. 'Circumcision in the Sudan.' *Middle East* (Mar. 1978). (Also in *WIN News* 4, 2 (Spring 1978):45.)

1443. 'A Woman's Place . . . Excerpts from Sudanow.' *WIN News* 4, 3 (Summer 1978):51–52.

1444. 'Women and Work in the Sudan.' Paper presented at

the National Congress of Sudanese Women's
Union, 20–24 Apr., 1976. *WIN News* 2, 4 (Autumn
1976):54.

1445. Zenkovsky, Sophie. 'Marriage Customs in Omdurman.'
Sudan Notes and Records 26 (1945): 241–255.

SYRIA

1446. Abdallah, Saad S. *Syrian Women and Syrian Women
Association*. Damascus, 1968.

1447. Allan, Donald. 'Syria's Women Volunteers: a Force for
Development.' *UNICEF News* no. 82 (1974):21–24.

1448. Bishtawi, A. 'Syrian Women and the International
Women's Year.' *Flash of Damascus* no. 43 (May
1975):12–19.

1449. Chatila, Khaled. *Le mariage chez les musulmans en
Syrie*. Paris: Presses Modernes, 1933.

1450. El-Daghestani, Kazim. *Etudes sociologiques sur la femme
musulmane en Syrie*. Paris: Leroux, 1932.

1451. 'L'éducation des femmes en Syrie.' *Open Court* (1932).

1452. Hilmi, M. 'The Changing Role of the Syrian Women
in the Labour Force.' Paper presented at the 9th
Annual Convention of the Association of the
Arab-American University Graduates, New York,
1–3 Oct., 1976.

1453. ILO. Office of Public Information. 'Syria: Carpets for
Better Living.' *ILO Panorama* no. 40 (Jan.–Feb.
1970).

1454. ILO. Technical Cooperation Report. 'Rapport au
gouvernement de la République Arabe Syrienne sur
la production de tapis en Syrie' (OIT/TAP/Syrie/
E.15). Geneva, 1970.

1455. Nallino, C.A. 'Mancata dimostrazione femminile contro
il velo a Damasco.' (Unsuccessful Demonstration
by Women in Damascus Against the Veil.) *Oriente
Moderno* 7, 10 (1927):492–493.

F

1456. Sakakini, Widad. 'The Evolution of Syrian Women.' *United Asian Journal* 1, 7 (1949):531–533.
1457. Thompson, Elizabeth Maria (Mrs. Bowen Thompson). *Daughters of Syria: a Narrative of Efforts of Mrs. Bowen Thompson for the Evangelization of the Syrian Females.* London: Seeley, 1872.
1458. Turjman, S. 'Syrian Women on the Way to Emancipation.' *Flash of Damascus* no. 5 (Nov. 1971):17–19.
1459. Vacca, V. 'Il congresso femminile a Damasco.' (Women's Congress at Damascus.) *Oriente Moderno* 10, 8 (1930):360–361.
1460. Vacca, V. 'Il congresso femminile siriano di Damasco.' (The Syrian Women's Congress at Damascus.) *Oriente Moderno* 12, 11 (1932):538–539.

TUNISIA

1461. Abu Zahra, Nadia. 'The Family in a Tunisian Village.' Paper presented at the Mediterranean Social, Anthropological and Sociological Conference, Nicosia, Cyprus, 7–12 Sept., 1970.
1462. Abul Naga, Attia S. 'L'émancipation de la femme en Tunisie.' *UN Special* no. 2 (1964):9–13.
1463. 'L'accession des femmes à l'emploi passe par des adaptations manuelles et mentales.' *La Presse*, 18 Feb. 1970.
1464. 'Adhésion de la Tunisie aux conventions internationales de Washington sur la condition de la femme.' *Revue de l'Institut des Belles Lettres Arabes* 31, 121/1 (1968):160.
1465. 'L'alphabétisation des femmes améliore l'environnement familial.' *L'Action*, 23 May, 1970.
1466. Ammar, S. and M'barek, E. 'L'hystérie chez la jeune fille et la femme tunisiennes.' *Tunisie Médicale* 4 (1961):12–27.

1467. Attia, Halima. 'Les statuts de la femme tunisienne au travail.' *Revue de Presse* (Jan. 1975):191.

1468. Auerbach, Elizabeth Stamen. 'Are Women in a Male Dominated Society Oppressed? An Analysis of the Role of Women in a Tunisian Town.' Paper presented at the American Anthropological Association, 72nd Annual Meeting, New Orleans, 28 Nov.–2 Dec., 1973.

1469. Baccar, Alia. 'Le thème de l'éducation de la jeune fille d'après les romanciers du XIXe siècle et d'après Zola en particulier.' *Les Cahiers de Tunisie* 22, 87–88 (1974):155–166.

1470. Balegh, H. 'Tunisie et mariage mixte.' *Hommes et Migrations: Documents* 12, 810 (July 1971):18–20.

1471. Ballet, J. 'Couture.' *Revue de l'Institut des Belles Lettres Arabes* 11, 3–4 (1948):373–376.

1472. Bchir, J., Bouraoui, A., Rouissi, M. and Zghal, A. 'L'influence sur le taux de fécondité du statut et du rôle de la femme dans la société tunisienne.' *Revue Tunisienne des Sciences Sociales* nos. 32–35 (1973).

1473. Becheur, A. 'La notion de grade dans le droit tunisien de la famille.' *Revue Algérienne des Sciences Juridiques, Economiques et Politiques* 5, 4 (Dec. 1968): 1149–60.

1474. Behar, L. 'Evolution récente de la nuptialité en Tunisie.' Tunis: National Office of Family Planning and Population, 1975. (Mimeographed.)

1475. Belgaid-Hassine, N. 'Motivations de la femme tunisienne au travail.' *Revue Tunisienne des Sciences Sociales* 4, 11 (Oct. 1967):85–95.

1476. Ben Ali, M. 'Les divorces en Tunisie.' Mémoire de fin d'études présenté devant l'Ecole Nationale de Service Social, Tunis, 1960.

1477. Ben Ammar, A. 'L'évolution de la famille en Tunisie et la réglementation actuelle du droit de garde.' *Hommes et Migration: Documents* 18, 695 (May 1967):1–7.

1478. Ben Ammar, A. 'La femme tunisienne à la croisée des chemins.' *Ath-Thouraya* (Aug.–Sept., Oct.–Nov. 1946).

1479. Benattar, R. 'Les conflits de juridiction en matière de divorce.' *Revue Tunisienne de Droit* (1968):25–44.

1480. Ben Brahem, S. 'La jeune tunisienne et le mariage.' *Jeune Afrique* no. 120 (Feb. 1963):25–27.

1481. Ben Salah, A. 'Si 25000 femmes voulaient.' *Faiza* 15 (May 1961):21–22.

1482. Ben Salah, M. 'Pour être libre, la femme doit être à la hauteur de ses responsabilités.' (Le Séminaire des Educatrices.) *La Presse*, 14 Apr., 1969.

1483. Berger, R. 'Die soziale Stellung der tunisischen Frau.' (Social Status of Tunisian Women.) Thesis, University of Fribourg, 1964.

1484. Berque, J. 'Pourquoi, chez la femme, la crise a éclaté maintenant et pas avant?' *Faiza* no. 56 (Mar.–Apr. 1967).

1485. Borrmans, Maurice. 'Code de statut personnel et évolution sociale en certains pays musulmans.' *Revue de l'Institut des Belles Lettres Arabes* 26, 103 (3ème trimestre 1963):205–259.

1486. Borrmans, Maurice. 'Deux études sur le divorce en Tunisie.' *Revue de l'Institut des Belles Lettres Arabes* 31, 122 (1968):255–294.

1487. Borrmans, Maurice. 'Le droit de garde (Hadana) et son évolution récente en Tunisie.' *Revue de l'Institut des Belles Lettres Arabes* 30 (1967):191–226.

1488. Boulic, J.Y. 'Sur le chemin de l'émancipation de la femme: à quoi rêvent jeunes tunisiennes?' *Croissance des Jeunes Nations* no. 118 (Dec. 1971):4–7.

1489. Bourguiba, Habib. 'Discourse à l'occasion de la fête de la femme.' *Action* (14 Aug., 1966).

1490. Bourguiba, Habib. *La femme: élément de progrés dans la société*. Tunisie: Sécrétariat d'Etat à l'Information et à l'Orientation, 13 Aug., 1965.

1491. Bourguiba, Habib. 'Il appartient à la femme de préparer l'avenir.' *La Presse*, 15 Aug., 1971.

1492. Bourguiba, Habib. 'Une priorité nationale: la réhabilitation de la femme et du mariage.' *Hommes et Migrations: Documents* 17, 671 (Nov. 1966). (Also in *Etudes Sociales Nord-Africaines*, 1966.)

1493. Bourguiba, Habib. 'Le voile.' *Femme* 4, 11 (1967): 16–17.

1494. Camilleri, Carmel. 'La femme tunisienne: représentation du statut et des rôles familiaux.' *Revue Française de Sociologie* 5, 3 (1964): 307–324.

1495. Camilleri, Carmel. 'Les jeunes gens tunisiens face au problème de la mixité.' *Confluent* 20 (Apr. 1962).

1496. Camilleri, Carmel. 'Les jeunes tunisiennes face au problème de la liberté de la jeune fille.' *Confluent* 7, 20 (Apr. 1962): 262–273.

1497. Camilleri, Carmel. *Jeunesse, famille et développement: essai sur le changement socio-culturel dans un pays du tiers monde (Tunisie).* Paris: Centre National de la Recherche Scientifique, 1973.

1498. Camilleri, Carmel. 'Modernity and the Family in Tunisia.' *Journal of Marriage and Family* 29 (1967): 590–595.

1499. Camilleri, Carmel. 'Statut et rôles familiaux de la femme: leur représentation dans les groupes de jeunes travailleuses tunisiennes.' *Revue Française de Sociologie* 5, 3 (July–Sept. 1964): 307–324.

1500. Caudio, A. *La révolution des femmes en Islam.* Paris: Julliard, 1957.

1501. Chabbi, B. 'Le mariage mixte.' *L'Etudiant Tunisien* (Apr. 1960).

1502. Charfi, Mohamed. 'Les conditions de forme du mariage en droit tunisien.' *Revue Tunisienne de Droit* (1969–1970): 11–38.

1503. Charfi, Mohamed. 'L'égalité entre l'homme et la femme dans le droit de la nationalité tunisienne.' *Revue Tunisienne de Droit* (1975): 73–86.

1504. Cherif, Selma. 'Le rôle de la musulmane tunisienne dans l'inadaptation sociale de l'enfant.' *Bulletin d'Information Sociale Tunisienne de Psychologie* no. 3 (1973): 10–14.

1505. De l'Ain, Girod. 'Tunisian Women.' *Le Monde*, 31 May, 1966, pp. 2–16.

1506. 'Débât sur la sexualité.' *Dialogue* no. 8 (Mar. 1976): 12–18.

1507. Demeerseman, A. 'L'évolution féminine tunisienne.' *Revue de l'Institut des Belles Lettres Arabes* 10 (1947): 221–236, 301–334. (Also in *Publications de l'Institut des Belles Lettres Arabes* 13 (1948): 52.)

1508. Demeerseman, A. *La famille tunisienne et les temps nouveaux.* Tunis: Maison Tunisienne de l'Edition, 1967.

1509. 'Le divorce à la tunisienne.' *Dialogue* no. 71 (Jan. 1976): 30–35.

1510. 'Dix ans de promotion féminine.' *Femme* no. 6 (1966): 5–60.

1511. Djedidi, S. 'L'évolution et la condition de la femme tunisienne et sa participation à la vie économique.' *L'Action*, 7 Nov., 1963.

1512. Donner, E. 'Comment je vois les tunisiennes.' *Faiza* no. 21 (Jan. 1962.)

1513. 'Douze femmes de la banlieue pauvre de Tunis donnent leur avis sur le contrôle des naissances.' *La Presse de Tunisie*, 22 Feb., 1963.

1514. 'The Education of Women: in Yugoslavia, in Tunisia, in India and in Cuba.' *Foreign Education Digest* 28, 1 (1963):41–49.

1515. 'L'émancipation de la femme.' *La Presse*, 14 Aug., 1971.

1516. Ennablia, Z. 'La tunisienne au travail.' *Faiza* no. 40 (1964).

1517. 'La femme et l'emploi.' *L'Action*, 16 May, 1970.

1518. 'La femme dans le temps et dans l'espace.' *La Presse*, 22 Aug., 1971.

1519. 'La femme tunisienne au travail: le mariage et les enfants sont-ils des obstacles sérieux au travail de la femme?' *La Presse*, 9 Apr., 1971.

1520. *La femme tunisienne et l'emploi.* Colloque de 8–11 Nov., 1966. Tunis: Institut Ali Bach Hamba, 1967.

1521. Fenniche, N. 'Attitudes des jeunes parents tunisois de 20 à 30 ans devant le mariage mixte.' *Revue Tunisienne des Sciences Sociales* no. 3 (June 1965).

1522. Ferchiou, S. 'Différentiation sexuelle de l'alimentation au Djerid (Tunisie).' *L'Homme* 8, 2 (1968):64–86.

1523. Fontaine, Jean. 'Situation de la femme écrivain en Tunisie.' *Extrait des Cahiers de Tunisie* 20, 79–80 (1972):285–307. (Also in *Zeitschrift der Deutschen Morgenländischen Gesellschaft* 124 Hft (1974).)

1524. Gaudin de Lagrance, E. 'Causes de divorce en Tunisie.'
      *Revue Algérienne des Sciences Juridiques, Econo-
      miques et Politiques* 5, 4 (1968):1109–1115.
1525. Grenier, Cynthia. 'Tunisia: Out from Behind the Veil.'
      Ms Magazine, Aug. 1974, pp. 88–91.
1526. Gwénolé, M. 'Femme et travail.' *Revue de l'Institut des
      Belles Lettres Arabes* 24 (1961):301–308.
1527. Haddad, Fatma. 'L'intégration de la femme tunisienne
      à la vie active.' Union Mondiale des Organismes
      pour la Sauvegarde de l'Enfance et de l'Adolescence,
      4ème Conférence Internationale, Tunis, 31 Mar.–
      6 Apr., 1969.
1528. Haddad, Radhia. 'L'action de l'Union Nationale des
      Femmes en Tunisie.' (U.N.F.T.) (Interview par
      Monique Harcha.) *Confluent* 7, 25 (1962):682–690.
1529. Hafsia, Jalila. 'La femme tunisienne au travail.' *La
      Presse*, 9 Apr., 1971.
1530. Hafsia, Nazli, 'La prostitution: un des couts de déve-
      loppement d'un pays sous-développé: Tunisie.'
      Thèse de 3e Cycle, Université de Tours, 1972.
1531. El-Hamamsy, Laila Shukry. *Assessment of UNICEF
      Assisted Projects for the Preparation and Training
      of Women and Girls for Community Development in
      Tunisia.* UNICEF document, Aug. 1969.
1532. Hammerton, Thomas. *Tunisia Unveiled.* London:
      Robert Hale, 1959.
1533. Harbi, M. 'L'émancipation de la femme entre l'insti-
      tution et la réalité.' *L'Action*, 13 Aug., 1971.
1534. Harcha, M. 'Les travailleuses sociales en Tunisie.'
      Revue de l'Institut des Belles Lettres Arabes 26,
      101/1 (1963):55–61.
1535. Hochschild, Arlie. 'Le travail des femmes dans une
      Tunisie en voie de modernisation: attitudes de
      jeunes filles en milieu urbain.' *Revue Tunisienne des
      Sciences Sociales* 4, 9 (Mar. 1967):145–166.
1536. Hochschild, Arlie. 'Women at Work at Modernizing
      Tunisia.' *Berkeley Journal of Sociology* II (1969):
      32–53.
1537. ILO. Office of Public Information. 'Assia—Girl of
      Tunis.' *ILO Panorama* (Jan.–Feb. 1968).

1538. ILO. Technical Cooperation Report. 'Project BIT/ SIDA Tunisie—centre national de formation professionnelle féminine.' Rapports semestriels no. 1/2, 1971/1972.

1539. ILO. Technical Cooperation Report. 'Rapport au Gouvernement de la Tunisie sur la préparation professionnelle de jeunes filles et des femmes en Tunisie.' (OIT/OTA/Tunisie/R.16), 1966.

1540. 'Il y a quatorze ans, la femme tunisienne accède à la dignité.' *L'Action*, 13 Aug., 1970.

1541. 'L'institutrice tunisienne.' *Femme* (15 Feb. 1969):26–29, 69–72.

1542. 'L'intégration de la femme tunisienne dans le monde du travail.' *La Presse*, 24 Nov., 1971.

1543. Jay, B. *et al.* 'Les familles mixtes en Tunisie.' Thèse de 3ème Cycle, Faculté de Théologie Protestante, Strasbourg, 1963.

1544. Jay, B. *et al.* 'Dossier confluent les mariages mixtes en Tunisie.' *Confluent* 35 (Nov. 1963).

1545. Ladislas, S.M. 'Réflexions sur l'éducation féminine tunisienne.' *Revue de l'Institut des Belles Lettres Arabes* 14 (1961):417–432.

1546. Lakehal-Ayat, Naziha. *La femme tunisienne et sa place dans le droit positif.* Tunis: Editions Dar el Amal, 1978.

1547. Lakhoua, Hédi. 'Reflexions sur le divorce "caprice".' *Revue Tunisienne de Droit* (1974):61–76.

1548. Larson, Barbara. 'Tunisian Women: a Veiled Threat.' Paper presented at the 7th Annual Meeting of the Middle East Studies Association, Milwaukee, Wis., 8–10 Nov., 1973.

1549. Liman, D. 'L'éducation de la femme en Tunisie: son évolution.' *Convergences* no. 2 (1969):70–72.

1550. Lelong, Michel. 'Femmes tunisiennes d'aujourd'hui.' *Revue de l'Institut des Belles Lettres Arabes* 22, 87 (3e trimestre 1959):354–357.

1551. Lelong Michel. 'La jeune fille de demain en Tunisie: une enquête de la revue *al-Ilham*.' *Revue de l'Institut des Belles Lettres Arabes* 18 (1955):357–362.

1552. Louis, I.A. and Sironval, M.M. 'Le mariage tradition-

nel en milieu berbère dans le sud de la Tunisie.'
Revue de l'Occident Musulman et de la Méditerranée
no. 12 (2e sem. 1972):93–121.

1553. Mabrouk, M. 'La femme en droit public tunisien.'
Revue de Presse (June–July 1974):186.

1554. Magnin, J. 'A propos de l'éducation de la fillette tunisienne.' *Revue de l'Institut des Belles Lettres Arabes*
5 (1942):298–313.

1555. 'Mariage en Tunisie en 1960.' *Bulletin de Statistiques et
d'Etudes Economiques* no. 17 (Jan.–Mar. 1962):
7–18.

1556. 'Mariage mixte.' *Revue de Presse* no. 79 (Nov. 1963).

1557. 'Les mariages mixtes en Tunisie.' *Confluent* 35 (1963):
855–878.

1558. 'Mariage mixtes: voir enquêtes du quotidien.' (Interview de la Présidente de l'Union Nationale des
Femmes en Tunisie (U.N.F.T.).) *La Presse* 9, 10,
11, 12 Jan., 1963.

1559. Mercury, Thérèse. 'La femme tunisienne au travail en
usine, aspects psychologiques et sociologiques.'
Thèse de 3e Cycle, Aix-en-Provence, 1969.

1560. 'Modification des articles 231 (prostitution) et 238
(adultère) du code de statut personnel. Voir enquête
de Souhayr Belhassen: adultère et prostitution ou
l'homme, la femme et la loi.' *Jeune Afrique* no. 375
(11–17 Mar., 1968):1–2.

1561. Montéty, Henri de. *Femmes de Tunisie*. Le Monde
d'Outre-Mer Passé et Présent, 3ème série, Essais
II. Paris: Mouton, 1958. (Also in *Hommes et
Migrations* no. 671 (23 Nov., 1966) and English
translation in *Middle East Journal* 11 (1957):
309–318.)

1562. Nassif, H. 'Women's Economic Roles in Developing
Tunisia.' Paper presented at the 9th Annual
Convention of the Association of the Arab-American University Graduates, New York, 1–3 Oct.,
1976.

1563. 'The New Women of Tunisia.' *Arab World* (Jan.–Feb.
1962):8–11.

1564. O'Barr, Jean. 'A Longitudinal Analysis of Political

Efficiency and Support Among Women and Men in Tunisia.' Paper presented at the Wellesley Conference on Women and Development, Wellesley College, Mass., 2–6 June, 1976.

1565. 'A l'occasion du 12e anniversaire de la promulgation du statut personnel.' *L'Action*, 13 Aug., 1968. (Also in *La Presse*, 14, 15, 16 Aug., 1968.)

1566. Pellegrin, A. 'L'évolution de la femme tunisienne.' *En Terre d'Islam* no. 16 (1941):231–246.

1567. 'Personalité de l'étudiante tunisienne.' *L'Etudiante Tunisienne* (Jan. 1960).

1568. 'La place de la femme dans la société tunisienne.' Tunis: Union Nationale des Femmes de Tunisie, 1976.

1569. Pruvost, Lucie. 'Condition juridique, politique et sociale de la femme: le 9e Congrès de l'Institut International de Droit d'Expression Française.' *Revue de l'Institut des Belles Lettres Arabes* 37, 134/2 (1974): 349–364.

1570. Pruvost, Lucie. 'La dot dans le code de statut personnel tunisien.' *Revue de l'Institut des Belles Lettres Arabes* 33, 126 (1970):265–281.

1571. Pruvost, Lucie. *Juriscasseur de droit comparé, V, Tunisie—Fascicule 1: Introduction générale, La famille* (31p.); *Fascicule 2: Incapacités, successions et libéralités, droit internationale privé* (33p.). Paris: Edition Technique, 1975.

1572. Pruvost, Lucie. 'Promotion de la femme et législation.' *Revue de l'Institut des Belles Lettres Arabes* 31, 122 (1968):347–355.

1573. Pruvost, Lucie. 'A propos de IVe Congrès de l'Union Nationale des Femmes en Tunisie.' *Revue de l'Institut des Belles Lettres Arabes* 29 (1966):439–447.

1574. Pruvost, Lucie. *La prostitution des mineures en Tunisie.* Tunis: Faculté de Droit, D.E.S. de Sciences Criminelles, 1973.

1575. Punch, Lea Anne. 'Le travail féminin et la formation professionnelle en Tunisie.' Paper presented at the Conference on La femme tunisienne et l'emploi, Tunis, 8–11 Nov., 1966.

1576. Sack, Richard. 'Education and Modernization in Tunisia: A Study on the Relationship between Education and Other Variables and Attitudinal Modernity.' Ph.D. dissertation, Stanford University, 1972.
1577. 'Shudder at the Knee, Banning the Miniskirt.' *Time*, 26 Aug., 1966, p. 26.
1578. Simmons, J., ed. 'Village and Family: Essays on Rural Tunisia.' *Middle East Journal* 30, 4 (1976):566–7.
1579. Slim, H. 'Note critique sur *Le Harem et les cousins* de G. Tillion.' *Revue Tunisienne des Sciences Sociales* 5, 12 (Jan. 1968).
1580. Stone, Russell and Simmons, J., eds. *Change in Tunisia.* Albany: State University of New York Press, 1976.
1581. Sugier, C. 'Les jeunes filles tunisiennes d'aujourd'hui.' *Revue de l'Institut des Belles Lettres Arabes* 19 (1956):233–239.
1582. Swedish International Development Authority. Research Division. *Women in Developing Countries— Case Studies of Six Countries* (Middle East and North Africa). Stockholm: SIDA, 1974.
1583. Tilli, N. 'L'aube du mouvement de réformes à Tunis: un important document de Ahmad Ibn-ad-Diyaf sur le féminisme (1856).' *Ethnie* 2 (1972):167–230.
1584. 'Le travail féminin face à l'opinion publique.' *L'Action*, 19, 26 Nov., 1967; 2, 8, 16 Dec., 1967.
1585. Tunisia. Sécrétariat d'Etat à l'Information. *La femme tunisienne.* 1960.
1586. 'La tunisienne et l'enseignement.' Enquête de *Faiza* nos. 21–25 (1962).
1587. UNESCO. 'National Inventory on the Place of Women in Tunisian Society' (ED-76/WS/74). Paris: UNESCO, 31 Dec., 1976.
1588. United Nations. FAO Programme. *The World Food Programme and Women's Involvement in Development.* Aug. 1975.
1589. United Nations. International Zone. *Women up in Arms.* McGraw-Hill: Contemporary Films, 1965. (28½ minutes in colour.)
1590. Union Nationale des Femmes Tunisiennes. *Aspects*

particuliers du problème de l'accés des femmes tunisiennes à l'éducation. Action de la Tunisie dans le domaine de l'éducation de la femme. n.d.

1591. Vallin, Jacques. 'La nuptialité en Tunisie.' *Population* (1971):250–266. (Special issue.)

1592. Van Den Heuven, S. (née Bouraoui). *Vie et formation de la jeune fille tunisienne de sa naissance à son adolescence.* Mémoire pédagogique pour le proféssorat d'enseignement secondaire, Université de Tunis, 1963.

1593. Vichniac, Isabelle. 'Assia, jeune fille de Tunis.' *Panorama de B.I.T.* no. 28 (Jan.–Feb. 1968): 16–21.

1594. World Student Christian Federation. 'The Educated Woman.' *Student World* 59, 3 (1966).

1595. Yotte, Yannick. 'La femme tunisienne dans son rôle de mère de famille.' *Culture* 2 (Winter 1970):6–12.

1596. Zghal, Abdel Kader. 'Classes sociales et identités culturelles dans le monde arabe musulman: le cas de la Tunisie.' Paper presented at the 9th World Congress of the International Political Science Association, Montreal, 1973.

1597. Zghal, Abdel Kader. 'Système de parenté et système coopératif dans les campagnes tunisiennes.' *Revue Tunisienne des Sciences Sociales* 4, 11 (Oct. 1967): 95–108.

UNITED ARAB EMIRATES

1598. Kergan, J.L. 'Social and Economic Changes in the Gulf Countries.' *Asian Affairs* 62 (New Series, Vol. 6, Part III) (Oct. 1975):282–289.

1599. 'Union of Arab Emirates.' *WIN News* 2 (Summer 1976):36.

1600. 'Women's Union Organization of the United Arab Emirates.' *WIN News* 2 (Autumn 1976):54.

YEMEN

1601. Beeston, A.F.L. 'The so-called Harlots of Hadramaut.'
    Oriens 5 (July 1952):16–22.
1602. Chelhod, Joseph. 'Les cérémonies du mariage au
    Yemen.' *Objets et Monde* 13, 1 (1973):3–34.
1603. Chelhod, Joseph. 'La parenté et le mariage au Yemen.'
    L'Ethnographie 67 (1973).
1604. Fayein, C. *Une française, médicin au Yemen.* Paris:
    Julliard, 1955.
1605. Gerlach, E. *Aus dem Harem in die Welt–Erlebnise unter
    den Frauen Südarabiens.* Leipzig: Brockhaus, 1962.
1606. Khalil, Fatimah Abdul Qawi. 'Indigenous Midwifery in
    Selected Villages in the Second Governorate of
    Peoples' Democratic Republic of Yemen.' M.A.
    thesis, American University of Beirut, Lebanon,
    1972.
1607. Makhlouf, Carla (Makhlouf-Obermeyer, Carla). 'Chan
    ging Women: the Case of North Yemen.' M.A.
    thesis, American University of Beirut, Lebanon,
    Nov., 1975.
1608. Makhlouf, Carla. *Changing Veils: a Study of Women in
    South Arabia.* London: Croom Helm, 1979;
    Austin: University of Texas Press, 1979.
1609. Myntti, Cynthia. 'Demographic Survey of Three
    Villages in the Yemen Arab Republic.' Ph.D.
    dissertation, London School of Economics, De-
    partment of Anthropology (forthcoming).
1610. Petran, Tabitha. 'South Yemen Ahead on Women's
    Rights.' *Middle East International* no. 48 (June
    1975):24–26.
1611. El-Sadr, Dawlat. *Girls' Education and Women Teacher
    Training, Yemen* (56/BMS.RD/EDS). Paris:
    UNESCO, 1967.
1612. Seranjan, B. 'The Sanaan Wedding; on Customs of the
    Yemenites.' *Aziz I Afrika* (Moscow) no. 6 (1962):
    53.

1613. Swanson, Rebecca L. 'Role of Women in the Yemen
       Arab Republic.' Washington, D.C.: Agency for
       International Development, 1975. (Mimeographed.)
1614. Wenner, M.W. *Modern Yemen*. Baltimore: Johns
       Hopkins University Press, 1967.
1615. 'Yemen Arab Republic: Women's Education for Rural
       Development.' *WIN News* 3 (Autumn 1977):60–61.
1616. 'Yemeni Women have come a Long Way from Feudal
       Past.' *International Herald Tribune*, 12 May,
       1979, p. 7.

Author Index

References are to entry numbers, and not to pages.

Aalami, S., 1047
Abass, A. de Zayas, 103
Abbott, Nadia, 104, 105, 1066
Abdallah, I.S., 335
Abdallah, Saad S., 1446
Abd Al-Razik, Ahmad, 906
Abdel Ati, Hammudah, 106
Abdel Fatah, Hoda, 336
Abdel Fateh, Kamilia, 907
Abdel Fattah, al Sayyid, 908
Abdel Hamid, Ibrahim, 107
Abdel Hamid, Naguiba, 337
Abdel Hamid, Najib, 975
Abdel Kader, Soha, 909, 910
Abdel Kafi, 1226
Abdel-Mahmoud, Fatima, 1395,
    1396, 1403
Abdel Rahman, Aisha, 108
Abdul, Khalik, 109
Abdul Qayyum, Shah, 911
Abdul Rauf, Mohammad, 111
    See also Rauf, M.A.
Aboutalib, Sofy, 213
Abou Zeid, Hekmat, 912
Abu-Abdallah, 782
Abu Daleb, Nuha, 1342
Abu Jaber, Faiz, 338
Abu Khadra, Rihab, 1136
Abu Laban, B., 470
Abul Naga, Attia S., 1462

Abu Lughod, Janet, 913
Abu Nasr, J., 1137
Abu Zahra, Nadia, 339, 340, 1461
Accad, Evelyn, 112, 341, 342,
    343, 344, 345, 720, 721, 783
Accad-Sursock, R., 1138
Acra-Amman, Katrin, 1139
Adams, John Boman, 914
Adams, Michael, 1
Adibe, N., 347
Adnane, L., 722
Afnan Shahid, Bahia, 1140
Afza, N., 113
Afzal, M., 114
Ahdab-Yehya, May, 348
Ahmed, Wajih, 349
El-Akel, Abderrazak, 116
Akolawin, N., 1397
Ali, M., 117, 118
Ali, Mukti, 119
Ali Parveen Shaukat, 120, 121
Alireza, Marianne, 1366
Aliyah, M.K. el Bindary, 916
Allan, Donald, 1447
Allman, James, 122
Alouche, R., 1141, 1142, 1143,
    1144
Alwaye, Mohieddin, 123
Al-Amin, A., 1238
Amin, Lucy, 913

Amine, R.G., 917
Al-Amir, Daisy, 350
Amiruddin, Begum Sultan Mir, 124
Ammar, S., 1466
Anastase Marie de St. Elie, 723
Anderson, J.N.D., 125, 126, 127, 128, 129, 130, 131, 351, 1067, 1089
Anderson, Norman, 132
El-Annabi, Tayyib, 724
Ansari, Ghaus, 352
Antoun, R.T., 2, 3, 353, 354
Aouissi, Cheikh Mechri, 786
Arab League, 357, 358, 359
Arafa, Bahiga, 918
El-Aref, Aref, 1343
Armand, M.L., 363
Arnaldez, Roger, 133
Arnaud, Gabriel, 787
Arnett, M.F., 919
Asad, Talal, 4
Asfar, Gabriel, 725
Aswad, B.C., 364
Attia, A., 1239
Attia, Halima, 1467
Auerbach, Elizabeth Stamen, 1468
Awad, B.A., 134
Awwad, Tawfiq Yusuf, 1146
Ayoub, M.R., 365, 366
Azzam, Henry, 367

Baali, F., 1068
Babaa, Khalid I., 368
Babazogli, S., 920
Babbitt, A.E., 1227
Baccar, Alia, 1469
Badawi, Gamal A., 135, 136
Badran, Aida, 137
Badran, Hoda, 138, 369, 370, 371, 372, 373, 921, 1367
Badran, Margot, 922
Baer, Gabriel, 5
Bagros, Sylvie, 1147
Baldwin, Stephen, 374
Balegh, H., 1470

Le Balle, R., 923
Ballet, J., 1471
Balley, C., 924
Bannaga, Ali Mohayad, 1398
Barbot, M., 375
Barhoum, Mohammad Issa, 1090, 1091
Baron, A.M., 1240
Baroudy, A., 139
Barrire, G., 788
Barth, Fredrik, 1069
Barzilai, S., 1344
Bashshur, Munir, 376
Bassyouni, A., 612
Bastide, Henri de la, 1241
Bateson, M.C., 377
Baveja, Malik R., 140
Bay, E.J., 749
El Baymoumi, Soheir, 925
Bayoudh, Edma, 1148, 1149
Bayoumi, Ahmed, 1399
Bayyuni, M.A.M., 926
Bchir, J., 1472
Bchir, M., 47
Bean, Lee L., 114
Bearani, H.S., 141
Beauvoir, Simone de, 789
Becheur, A., 1473
Beck, Dorothy Fahs, 379
Beck, Lois, 142, 143, 378
Beeston, A.F.L., 1601
Behar, L., 1474
Beirut University College, 1150
Belgaid-Hassine, N., 1475
Belghiti, Malika, 1242, 1243, 1244
Belmihoud, M., 794
Ben Abdalla, 144
Benabed, H.H., 145
Ben Ali, M., 1476
Ben-Ami, Issachar, 1245
Ben Ammar, A., 1477, 1478
Benatia, Farouk, 790, 791, 792
Benatia, M., 793
Benattar, R., 1479
Ben Brahem, S., 1480
Benhadji Serradj, M., 1246
Bennani, Mesdal, 1247

Ben Salah, A., 1481
Ben Salah, M., 1482
Bentami, Rosalie, 726
Berger, Morroe, 6, 7, 380
Berger, R., 1483
Berhnheim, N., 1248
Berlas, N.H., 146
Berque, Jacques, 8, 1484
Bexter, C.B., 927
Bezirgan, Basima, 444, 445
Bickers, William, 381
Bindary, Aziza, 927
Bint al Shati' (Aisha Abdel
  Rahman), 147
Bishtawi, A., 1448
Bitat, Zohra, 794
Bittari, Zoubeida, 148
Blanc, A., 795
Blanch, Lesley, 382, 383
Boals, Kathryn, 796
Boals, Kay, 797, 798
Bohdanowicz, Arslan, 928
Boissenot, 799
Bolo, Etienne, 1249
Bonnet-Eymard, J., 149
Borrmans, Maurice, 150, 728,
  800, 1250, 1485, 1486, 1487
Boserup, Ester, 384, 385, 386, 387
Boss, Mary, 388
Boubakeaur, H., 729
Boubaker, F., 801
Bouhdiba, Abdel Wahab, 151,
  152, 153, 389
Boulic, J.Y., 1488
Boullata, Kamal, 390
Bourguiba, Habib, 1489, 1490,
  1491, 1492, 1493
Bousquet, George-Henri, 154,
  155, 156, 157, 803, 804
Bousquet-Lefèvre, L., 802
Bousser, M., 1251
Boutarfa, Salah el-Dine, 393
Boutémène, Yahia, 805
Brom, Kenneth, 1252
Brunschvig, R., 158
Budiner, Melitta, 391
Burhil, Zoubaida, 392
Bujra, Abdallah, 394

Burton, Richard, 9, 10
Bushakra, Mary, 1151
El-Bustan, Afifa I., 1070
Butti, Rufail, 1071
Buttin, P., 1253

Cairo Family Planning
  Association, 929
El-Calamawy, Suhair, 930
Calame-Griaule, G., 1400
Callens, M., 730
Calverley, Eleanor J., 1116
Camilleri, Carmel, 1494, 1495,
  1496, 1497, 1498, 1499
Canaan, T., 1345
Carol, Jacqueline, 931
Castagné, J., 159
Castillo, Gelia T., 395
Catrice, Paul, 396
Caudio, A., 1500
Cazautets, J., 1254
Celarié, Henriette, 1255
Centre d'Études et de Recherches
  Démographiques, 1256, 1257
Centre d'Études pour le Monde
  Arabe Moderne, 160
Chabaud, Jacqueline, 397
Chabbi, B., 1501
Chamberlayne, J., 161
Chambers, R., 40
Chamie, Mary, 1152, 1153
Chamla, Marie-Claude, 806
Chamoun, Mounir, 1154, 1155,
  1156, 1195
Chapoutot-Remadi, M., 398
Charaoui, G., 933
Charara, Yolla Polity, 1157,
  1158, 1159
Charfi, Mohamed, 1502, 1503
Charnay, Jean-Paul, 11, 162, 399,
  400, 401, 1258
Charroin, J., 807
Chatila, Khaled, 1449
Chebat, Fouad, 402
Chehab, Leila, 1160
Chehata, Chafik, 163, 164, 165
Chelhod, Joseph, 166, 403, 1117,
  1387, 1602, 1603

Chemali, Mona, 404
Cherif, Selma, 1504
Chidiac, M., 1161
Chkounda, H., 1261
Chraibi, Najat, 1246
Churchill, C.W., 29
Citrine, Malika, 167
Clark, Isobel, 1401
Clifford, Mary Louise, 1368
Clignet, R., 405
Cogswell, B.E., 12
Cohen, R., 168
Cole, Donald, 1369
Columbia Human Rights
  Review, 934
Contu, Giuseppe, 935
Cooper, Elizabeth, 409, 936
Corrèze, F., 808
Corti, Ghannam L., 171
Coulson, N.J., 172
Crabitis, P., 173
Crapanzano, V., 410
Cuisenier, Jean, 411
Cunnison, Ian, 1402

El-Daghestani, Kazem, 412, 1450
Daguin, A., 732
D'Ancezune, H. Rostan, 1145
Danforth, Sandra, 413
Daoud, Z. al Achgar, 1261
Darwish, Y.H., 414
Daumas, Général, 415
Daura, Bello, 177
Davies, A.M., 1344
Davis, J., 13
Davis, J.L.R., 428
Davis, Susan S., 416, 1262, 1263,
  1264
Dearden, Ann, 1370
Debèche, Djamila, 178, 179, 180,
  810, 811, 812
Debs, Richard A., 937
Decrop, M., 1265
Decroux, Paul, 181, 417, 1266
Deeb, Mary Jane A., 1162
Dejeux, J., 813, 814
De l'Ain, Girod, 1505
De Lauwe, P.-H., 418

De Marchi, M., 1083
Demeerseman, A., 419, 1507,
  1508
Demoulin, F., 806
Denison, S.M., 733
Denneth, Charlotte, 1163
Deonna, Laurence, 420
Deprez, J., 1267
Desanti, Dominique, 421, 734
Desportes, E., 182, 183, 735
Despres, L., 736
Des Villettes, J., 1164
Devereux, Robert, 184
Devos, George, 865
Devulder, M., 737
Diab, Lutfi, 41, 42
Diaz, Christina, 1401
Dickson, H.R.P., 1118
Dickson, Violet, 1119
Di Napoli, George, S.J., 1199
Dionisi, Bianca, 815
Dixon, Ruth B., 422
Djebar, Assia, 186
Djedidi, S., 1511
Dodd, Peter, 423, 424, 425, 938
Dodd, Stuart Carter, 14
Donaldson, D.M., 187
Donner, E., 1512
Dostal, W., 426
Douedar, Marysa, 818
Douglas, Joseph, 940
Douglas, K.W., 940
Doumergue, G., 739
Dowaicher, Safia M., 897
Drower, E.S., 1072
Duchac, J., 1268
Dughi, N., 1269
Duverger, M., 427
Duvignaud, Jean, 740
Dwyer, Daisy, 1270, 1271, 1272,
  1273, 1274

Eekelaar, J.M., 428
Ehrenfels, U.R., 188, 189
Eickelman, Dale F., 1276
Elwan, Shwikar, 429
Ennablia, Z., 1516
Ergunduz, Mirgun, 430

Esposito, J.L., 190, 191, 192, 951
Estivals, G., 819
El-Eteify, Gamal, 431
Etienne, B., 742, 820
Evans-Pritchard, Edward, 432, 743

Fadlallah, I., 404
Faffler, Irene, 433
Fahmi, Aisha, 434
Fahmi, Noha, 435
Fahmy, Hoda, 952
Fahmy, M., 193
Faivre, Charles, 822
Fakhouri, H., 953
Farber, M.A., 436
Farman-Farmaian, Sattareh, 194
Farrag, A.M., 954
Farrag, Amina, 823
Farrag, O.L., 195, 437
Farran, C. d'Olivier, 1404
Farsoun, K., 1167
Farsoun, Samih K., 1166, 1167
Al-Faruqi, L., 438
Al-Faruqi, Lamia, 196
El-Fasi, Mohammad, 1277
Fattal, Antoine, 197
Fauque, L.P., 824, 825, 826
Fawzi, S., 1405
Fayein, C., 1604
Fedorova, Zinaida, 1347
Fenniche, N., 1521
Ferchiou, S., 1522
Fergany, Nader, 442, 955
Fernande, Lucas, 746
Fernea, Elizabeth, 443, 444, 445, 446, 447, 1073, 1279
Fernea, Robert, 956, 1074
Fikry, M., 1228
Fisher, Sydney N., 16
Fitch, Florence, 1348
Fletcher, David, 1121
Flory, Vera E., 201
Fluehr-Lobban, Carolyn, 448, 449, 450, 1406, 1407, 1408, 1409, 1410
Foca, R., 202

Fontaine, C., 747
Fontaine, Jean, 1523
Forget, Nelly, 1280
Foudil, Abdel Kadir, 831
Fox, Greer, L., 451
Francisi, A., 1281, 1411
François, S.M., 832
Francos, Anya, 748
Freeth, Zahra, 1122
Fuleihan, Louise, 453
Fuller, Anne H., 1169

Galenson, Marjorie, 454
Galtier, F., 455
Gannagé, Pierre, 17
El-Garh, M., 203
Gaudin de Lagrance, E., 1524
Gaudio, Attilio, 204
Gaudry, Mathéa, 834, 835, 836
Gauthier, E.F., 205
Geargoura, Christian, 957
Geertz, Clifford, 206
General Federation of Iraqi Women, 1075
General Union of Palestine Women, 1349
Geniaux, C., 207
Gentric, H., 1282
George, Alan, 1232
Gerlach, E., 1605
Germanos-Ghazaly, L., 1170
Germanus, Julius, 456
Gharzouzi, Eva, 958
El-Ghonemy, M.R., 457
Ghorayyib, Rose, 1149
Gibb, H.A.R., 208, 209
Giele, J., 620
Giele, J.Z., 458, 959
Giffen, L.A., 459
Gifoun, N., 1412
Gillet, M., 325
Giuliani, V., 1413
Giuseppe, Gabriel, 460
Goichon, A.M., 837, 1283
Goldziher, Ignaz, 461
Goody, J.R., 462
Gordon, David, 838
Gornick, Vivian, 960

Graff-Wassink, M.W., 1284
Granada-Dewey, J., 961
Granqvist, Hilma, 1350, 1351
Graziani, J., 211, 463
Greene, Marilyn, 899
Greiss, S.E., 962
Grenier, Cynthia, 1525
Grimal, Pierre, 464
Gruyther, L., 465
Gulick, John, 18
Gwénolé, M., 1526

Haddad, Fatma, 1527
Haddad, Radhia, 1528
Al-Haddad, Tahir, 212
Haddad, William, 213, 466
Haddad, Y., 309
Haddad, Yvonne, 214, 309
Hafkin, Nancy J., 749
Hafsia, Jalila, 1529
Hafsia, Nazli, 1530
Haikal, A., 963
Al-Haj, F.M., 467
Haji Elmi, Mariam, 1390
Hajjar, Raja, 468
Halimi, Gisèle, 469, 789
Hamady, Sania, 19
Hamalian, Arpi, 1171, 1172
El-Hamamsy, Laila, 750, 751,
    964, 965, 1531
Hambert, W.W., 547
Hamdan, Hussein, 1173
Al-Hamdani, M., 470
Hamid, H.A., 215
Hammerton, Thomas, 1532
Hammond, Dorothy, 20, 21, 22
Hanania, Edith, 471
Hansen, Henry H., 900, 901, 966,
    1076
Harbi, M., 1533
Harcha, M., 1534
Harfouche, Jamal Karam, 1174
Haroun, Mohammad Ali, 839
Harry, Myriam, 472
Hartmann, M., 216
Hasan, Masud, 217
Hashim, A., 218
Hassar, F., 1285

Al-Hassar, M., 1286
El-Hassar-Zeghari, Latifa, 1287
Hatab, Zuhair, 23
Hayes, H.E.E., 219
Hayes, Rose Oldfield, 1414
Hazou, Micheline, 1175
Heard-Bey, F., 1338
Heeren, F., 247
Heggoy, Alf Andrew, 840, 841,
    842
Henin, R.A., 1415
Hennebelle, G., 843
Hickey, Margaret, 473
Hilal, Jamil, 474, 475
Hillary, Myall St. Joseph, 476
Hilmi, M., 1452
Hinchcliffe, D., 220
Hirabayashi, Gordon, 1093
Hobbalah, M., 221
Hochschild, Arlie, 1535, 1536
Hoffman, Bernard G., 1288
Hofmann, I., 1416
Holler, Joanne, 24
Hollingsworth, T.H., 927
Holtzclaw, Katherine, 967
Honoré-Laine, G., 844
Hopwood, D., 1373
Horis, S., 968
Hosken, Franziska P., 752, 1391
Hourani, Furugh, 477
Howard, I., 222
Howe, Sonia, 845
Howell, D., 1176
Hume-Griffith, M.E., 478
Husain, I., 114
Hussain, Muhammad, 223
Hussein, Aziza, 224, 225, 479,
    480, 969, 970, 971, 972, 973,
    974, 975
Hussein, P.H., 976
Huston, Perdita, 481, 753, 754

Ibrahim, Laila, 1418
Ibn Hazm, Abu Muhammad, 482
Ibn ou Alfourat, 226
Idris, H.R., 227, 228
Iglitzin, Lynne B., 483
ILO, 485, 486, 487, 846, 1454

ILO. Office of Public
Information, 1236, 1453, 1537,
1538, 1539
Ingrams, Doreen, 488
Institute for Women's Studies in
the Arab World, 489
International Bank for
Reconstruction and
Development, 490
International Federation of
Business and Professional
Women, 491
Iraq. Ministry of Social Affairs
and Labour, 1077
Al-Isa, M., 493
Ismail, S.K., 492
Issad, Mohand, 847
Izzeddin, Najla, 26
Izzeddine, Randa, 495

Jablow, Alto, 20
Jabra, Nancy, 1178
Jabri, Pearl, 496
Jacob, J.A., 497
Jacobs, Milton, 1289
Jacobs, S.E., 498
Jafarey, S.A., 1352
Jahier, H., 157
Jamali, S.F., 499
Jameelah, Maryam, 230
Jamous, R., 500
Jansen, M.E., 501
Jay, B., 1543, 1544
El-Jazouli, N., 1290
Jennings, R.C., 231
Jessup, H.H., 502
Johnston, Margaret L., 503
Joly, Gertrude, 1179
Jomier, J., 504
Jordan. Ministry of Labor.
Department of Women's
Affairs, 1095, 1096
Joseph, S., 446
Joseph, Suad, 1180, 1181
Joubin, Odette, 755
Joyce, Thomas, 505

Kallab, Ilham, 1182

Kamel, Abdel Aziz, 232
Kandis, Afaf Deeb, 1098
Karmi, H.S., 233
El-Karmy, Nada, 1353
Karoui Chabbi, Belgacem, 234
El-Kassir, Maliha, 1078, 1079,
1080, 1081
Katakura, Motoko, 1374
Katz, Naomi, 506, 507
Kawar, Widad, 1363
Keddie, Nikki, 143, 235, 378, 508,
509
Keenan, Jeremy, 851, 852
Kergan, J.L., 1598
Kendall, E.M., 1419
Kennedy, J.G., 978
Kesler, S.W., 510
Keyser, J., 511
Khal, Helen, 1183
Khalaf, Samir, 1184, 1185, 1186
Khalafallah, M.A., 236
Al-Khalidi, Anbara, 512
Khalifa, Ahmed M., 979
Khalil, Fatimah Abdul Qawi,
1606
Khalil, Rasmiya, 513
Khayat, Abdel Aziz, 237
Khayo, Mary, 1099
Khayreya, Anwar, 1420
Khayri, Majduddin Omar, 1100,
1101
El-Khayyat, G., 514
Khayyat, Latif, 1082
Khellad, A., 1251
Khuda Bakhsh, S., 515
Khuri, Fuad, 516, 1187
Kirkpatrick, J.S., 854
Klein, Viola, 517, 518
Kongstad, P., 1186
Korson, J.H., 238
Koura, Salah-Eddine, 855
Krachkovsky, I.Y., 980
Kramer, J., 410
Kupinsky, Stanley, 519
Kuwait. Central Statistics Office,
1124
Kuwait. Family Development
Society, 1125

Kuwait. Ministère des Affaires
Sociales et du Travail, 1126
Kuwait. Ministry of Education,
1127, 1128
Kuwait. Ministry of Social
Affairs and Labour, 1129
Kuwait. Permanent Mission of
the State of Kuwait to the
UN, 1130

Ladislas, S.M., 1545
Lahlou, Abbes, 1291, 1292
Lahoud, Aline, 1188
Laidlaw, R.G.B., 520
Laine, Geneviève, 856
Lakehal-Ayat, Naziha, 1546
Lakhoua, Hédi, 1547
Lallement, Ann-Marie, 1293
Lammens, H., 239
Lamphere, L., 588
Lamsa, George M., 521
Lane, E.W., 981
Lane-Poole, Stanley, 27
Lapanne-Joinville, J., 240, 241,
242, 243
Lapham, Robert, 1294, 1295
Larguesche, H., 244
Larsen, P., 522
Larson, Barbara, 1548
Layish, Aharon, 245, 246
Layson, H., 523
Lecomte, Jean, 1296
Lefèbvre, G., 857, 858
Legassick, T., 524
Lehrman, Hal, 525
Lelong, Michel, 1550, 1551
Lemanski, W., 526
Lemu, Aisha, 247
Lerner, Daniel, 28
Lesley, Blanche, 527
Leslie, Doris, 528
Levy, Reuben, 248
Lewis, F., 859
Lewis, I.M., 1393
Libya. Ministry of Education,
1229
Lichtenstadter, Ilse, 529, 983,
984, 985

Liljencrantz, C., 387
Liman, D., 1549
Lockyer, Herbert, 530
Lodi, Z., 249
Lofts, N., 531
Lorear, A., 250
Lorfing, Irene, 1199
Louis, I.A., 1552
Lowenfels, A.B., 763
Loya, Arieh, 532
Lucas, F., 756
Lucman, T.A., 251
Lunt, James, 1102
Lutfiyya, Abdulla M., 29, 1103

Mabrouk, M., 1553
Macdonald-Fahey, P., 533
McGrath, Patricia, 540
Macleod, R.B., 30
Maghraby, Marlene, 986
Magnin, J., 1554
Maher, Vanessa, 1297, 1298, 1299
Mahmoud, Fatma B., 1421
Makarius, Raoul, 534
Makhlouf, Carla, 1607, 1608
Malhas, Thurayya, 252
Malik, F.H., 253
Malika, Cirrine, 254
Malka, Elie, 1300
Mallah, M.A., 1105
Manniche, L., 987
Mansour, Sylvie, 1355
Marchand, Henri, 860, 861
Marchant, A., 862
Marmey, P., 864
Marmorstein, Emile, 535
Marshall, John F., 31
Martenson, Mona, 1301
Marx, E.E., 1356
Mason, John Paul, 1231
Al Masry, Youssef, 536
Mathews, Basil, 537
Matthiasson, Carolyn J., 538
Maudidi, S., 256
Mazas, P., 1190
Mazumdar, V., 539
M'barek, E., 1466
Mead, Richard, 1232

Melconian, Marlene, 541
Meleis, Afaf, 1131
Melikian, Levon, 542, 543
Mendelsohn, Micaela, 546
Mendo, C.R., 1302
Mercer, Dennis, 1339
Mercury, Thérèse, 1559
Mernissi, Fatima, 544, 545, 595,
    1303, 1304, 1305, 1306, 1307,
    1308
Merriam, K.H., 451, 988, 989
Miéville, W., 990
Mikhail, Mona, 758
Miladi, Khadija, 1233
Miller, Kaity, 546
Milton, Nancy, 506, 507
Miner, H., 865
Minturn, L., 547
Mirshak, Myra, 548, 1191, 1192,
    1193
Mitchell, Loretta, 991
Mito, Mohammad Abdel
    Moneim S., 992
Mogannam, Matiel, 549, 1357
Mohamed, Ahmed Zaki, 257
Mohamed, Hafez M., 994
Mohanna, Ahmed I., 258
Mohsen, A., 550
Mohsen, Safia, 551
Mokarzel, S.A., 759
Molinari, 1309
Montagne, Joel, 1296
Monteil, Vincent, 259, 260
Montéty, Henri de, 1561
Moore, Kate, 642
Morris, C.L., 1312
Morsey, Magaly, 1313
Morton, H.V., 552
Moukaddem, Tuaam R., 1194
Mourani, H., 1195
M'rabet, Fadela, 866, 867
El-Mufty, E., 1104
Muhyi, I.A., 553
Mulliken, Frances, 554
Murphy, Robert, 555
Musil, Alois, 1375
Mustaffa-Kedah, O., 556, 557
Al-Mu'tasim, M., 995

Myntti, Cynthia, 1609

Nabraoui, C., 996, 997, 998, 999
Nadim, Nawal el Messiri, 1000,
    1001
Nagi, Moustafa H., 1002, 1003
Nahas, K., 558
Nahas, M.K., 32
Najarian, Pergouhi, 33
Najjar, Mona, 559
Najjar, S., 1196
Najmun Nisa, Begum, 560
Nallino, C.A., 263, 1004, 1455
Nallino, M., 1197
Narbeth, E.G., 868
Naser, Abdullah Omar, 561
Nasir, Sari J., 1106
Nassif, H., 1562
Nath, Kamla, 1132
National Council of Lebanese
    Women, 264
Nazat, Afra, 265
Neal, Shirley, 266
Nejjari, F., 267
Nelson, Cynthia, 563, 564, 565,
    566, 1005, 1006
Nerval, G. de, 1007
Newsland, Kathleen, 567
Niazi, Kausar, 268, 269, 270, 271
Nijim, Basheer, 1234
Nolte, Richard H., 34
Norés, E., 272
Northcott, L.C., 1008
Nouacer, Khadidja, 1315, 1316
Nuwayri, Jumana, 1198
Nyland, P., 273

O'Barr, Jean, 568, 569, 1564
Oden, R.A., 570

Palmer, Ingrid, 573
Palmer, M.R., 1009
Paolini, John, 761
Papanek, Hanna, 274
Paret, R., 574
Partington, M., 575
Pastner, Carroll, 275, 276
Patai, Raphael, 35, 36, 576, 577,
    578

Patron, M., 1269
Paulme, Denise, 762
Peale, Octave, 277
Pellegrin, A., 1566
Penzer, N.M., 579
Peristiany, J.G., 37, 38, 39
Perlmann, M., 1010
Pestalozza, Uberto, 580
Peters, Emrys, 581, 582
Petersen, Karen Kay, 1011
Petran, Tabitha, 1610
Phares, Dr. Joseph, 1199
Philipp, T., 583
Phillips, Daisy George, 1012, 1013
Pierre, R., 1014
Piesse, Louis, 584
Pieters, Guy, 763
Pittman, C.R., 278
Polgar, Steven, 31
Polk, William, 40
Portier, L., 870
Prothro, E.T., 41, 42, 543, 1200
Pruvost, Lucie, 1569, 1570, 1571, 1572, 1573, 1574
Punch, Lea Anne, 1575

Qadri, M.S.A., 279
Qadry, Hind Tahsin, 1084
Qattan, Basima, 447
Al-Qazzaz, A., 585
Qutub, Ishaq, 1108

Rafiq, B.A., 280
Rafiullah, Abu Shihab, 281
Rahmatallah, Malleeha, 1085
Ramadan, Said, 282
Ramzi, Nahed, 435
Raphael, Dana, 43
Rashed, Fatma M., 1015
Rashed, Zeinab, 283
Rasheed, Bahega, S., 1016
Rassam, Amal (Vinogradov, Amal Rassam), 1320, 1321, 1322
Rauf, M.A., 284
Raza, M., 286
Reintjens, Hortense, 1377

Rejwan, Nissim, 285
Reza-ur-Rahim, 287
Richards, G.E., 1422
Rivlin, Benjamin, 44
Rizk, Hanna, 1109
Roberds, Frances E., 765
Roberts, Robert, 288
Roche, M.H., 871
Rodriguez Mellado, I., 1017
Rohlich-Leavitt, Ruby, 587
Rondot, Pierre, 45
Roques, Prete, 766
Rosaldo, M., 588
Rosen, Lawrence, 289
Rosenfeld, Henry, 46, 589
Rosenthal, Franz, 290
Ross, Mary, 1018
Rossi, E., 291, 1019, 1020, 1021
Rouhani, Dr., 292
Rouissi, M., 47
Roussier, Jules, 873, 874, 875, 876
Royere, Jean, 590
Rubeiz, Ghassan, 591, 592, 593
Rushdi Pacha, Mme (Niya Salima), 1022
Rynty, Carol J., 294

Saab, Edouard, 594
Saad, Mahasin, 1424
Sa'ad, N.M., 1378
Sabri, Marie A., 1201
Sabri, Munira, 1023
Sack, Richard, 1576
Sadat, Jihan, 1024
Sadawi, Nawal, 595
El-Sadr, Dawlat, 1611
Safilios-Rothschild, C., 596, 597, 598
Safwad, Osman, 295
Es-Said, Nimra Tannous, 599, 1110, 1111, 1112, 1113, 1114
Sakakini, Doria, 1025
Sakakini, Widad, 1456
Saleh, Saneya, 296, 297, 298, 1026
Saleh, Sheikh Subhi, 299
Salman, A.M.M., 300

Salman, Sylvia, 600
Salts, Margaret, 554
Samman, M.I., 1027
El Samaan, N.J., 601
Sammari, Mohammad S.R., 301
El-Sanabary, N., 602, 603, 604
Sanderson, Lilian, 1425, 1426, 1427
Saudi Arabia. Permanent Mission to the UN, 1380
Saunders, Lucie W., 1029
El-Sawi, Shahera, 1030
El-Sayed, D.H., 302
Sayegh, Rosemary, 605
Sayegh, Salma, 1202
Sbaity, Fatima, 1203
Schacht, J., 303
Schaefer, Davis Susan, 1323
Schlegel, Alice, 606
Schneider, Jane, 607
Schoen, C., 877
Sebban-Khan, A., 1360
Seilbert, Ilse, 608
Seklani, M., 47, 609
Selosse, J., 1324
Senfeld, Henry, 610
Seranjan, B., 1612
Shafie, Erfan, 612
Shafik, Doria, 1031, 1032, 1033, 1034, 1035
Shahid, Bahia Afnan, 1204
Shaltout, Mahmoud, 304, 305
Shammout, A., 1381
El Shamy, Hassan, 1028
Shanan, Naadirah, 306
Shandall, A. Abdul Futuh, 1428
Sheik-ul-Din, Dina, 1429
Shepherd, E.R., 307
Sherbini, Isabel, 1036
Shilling, Nancy A., 614
Shiloh, Ailon, 48
Shukri, Ahmed, 619
Siddiqui, M.M., 308
Sidhom, Samiha, 1037
Siham, B., 1038
Simmons, J., 1578, 1580
Sims, O.S., 618
Singh, Jyoti, 684, 685

Singletary, James, 617
Sironval, M.M., 1552
Skarzynska, K., 767
Slim, H., 1579
Smith, J., 309
Smith, Margaret, 310, 1430
Smith, Page, 615
Smith, William Robertson, 586, 616
Smock, Audrey C., 458, 620, 959
Soorma, C.A., 311
Soueif, M.I., 1039
Sourial, Aida Fahmy, 1040
Souriau, C., 1235
Spelman, N.G., 1431
Spencer, Robert, 622
Stern, Gertrude H., 312
Stiehm, Judith H., 768, 797, 798, 881
Stillman, Yedida K., 1042
Stoltzfus, W.A., 623
Stone, Russell, 1580
Stuers, Cora Vreede-de, 1133
Sudan. Ministry of Education, 1433
Sugier, C., 1581
Sukhdev Singh, 313
Sukkarieh, Bassimah Elias, 1205
Sukkary, Suheir, 1043
Suleiman, Michael W., 1044
Suliman, Salma M., 1437
Sussman, H.B., 12
Swan, G., 314
Swanson, Rebecca L., 1613
Swedish International Development Authority, 1582
Sweet, Louise, 49, 1206, 1207
Szyliowicz, J., 44, 50

Taalbi, M., 315, 50
Tabbara, Sajida, 316
Tabesh, Intisar, 624
Tabutin, Dominique, 882
Taha, H. M., 434
Taki, Ali Hassan, 903, 904
Talbi, Mohieddin, 51
Al-Talib, N., 626
Tambiah, S.J., 462

Tannous, Nimra (Es-Said, Nimra
Tannous), 627
Tapper, Nancy, 628
Tarazi, M.F., 629
Tarcici, A., 1208
Tawil, Ramonda, 1361
Tawile, Maurice, 1209
Technical Assistance Information
Clearing House, 625
Al-Thakeb, Fahad T., 1134
Thompson, A.Y., 1045
Thompson, Carolyn A., 377
Thompson, D., 1382
Thompson, Elizabeth Maria
(Mrs. Bowen Thompson), 1457
Thornburg, Max W., 53
Al-Tikriti, Y.H., 54
Tilli, N., 1583
Tillion, Germaine, 630, 631, 769,
1046
Timm, Klaus, 1047
Tinker, Irene, 632
Tobi, Anessa, 1327
Tomeh, Aida, 633, 634, 635, 636
637, 638, 639, 640, 1210
Tomiche, Nada, 1048, 1049,
1050, 1051
Al-Torki, Soraya, 641, 1383
Touat, L., 883
Touma, Toufic, 1211
Traini, R., 1384, 1385, 1386
Tubiana, J., 1439
Tuckwell, Sue, 642
Tunisia. Sécrétariat d'Etat à
l'Information, 1585
Turing, Penelope, 1115
Turjman, S., 1458
El-Turki, Ahmed M.A., 643, 644
Turton, Godfrey, 645

UNESCO, 55, 646, 647, 648, 649,
650, 651, 652, 653, 654, 655,
656, 1212, 1213, 1587
Ungor, Berait Zeki, 657
UNICEF, 658, 659, 660, 662,
662, 663, 1340
Union Nationale des Femmes
Tunisiennes, 1590

United Nations Development
Program, 904, 905
United Nations. Economic and
Social Council, 664, 665, 666,
667, 668, 669, 670, 1214, 1440
United Nations. Economic
Commission for Africa, 770,
771, 772, 773
United Nations. Economic
Commission for Western Asia,
56, 317, 671, 672, 673, 674, 675,
676, 774
United Nations. FAO
Programme, 1588
United Nations. International
Labour Organization, 677, 678
United Nations. International
Zone, 1589
United Nations. Office of Public
Information, 679, 680
United Nations. UNESOB, 318
United Nations. World Health
Organization, 102a, 775, 1215
Uplegger, H., 1328
Uzayzir, Z., 1387

Vacca, V., 319, 320, 682, 683,
1052, 1086, 1459, 1460
Vajrathon, Mallica, 595, 684,
685
Vallin Jacques, 884, 885, 886,
1591
Van Den Heuven, S., 1592
Van Dervort, T.R., 57
Van Dusen, Roxann A., 686,
687, 1216, 1217, 1218
Van Ess, Dorothy, 321
Van Nieuwenhuijze, C.A.O., 58,
59
Van Sommer, A., 322, 323
Vasse, Denis, 887
Vaucher-Zananiri, N., 1053,
1329
Veccia-Vaglieri, L., 324, 1054
Vernier, Pierre, 688, 689
Vexivière, J., 325
Vial, C., 1055
Vichniac, Isabelle, 1593

Vigier, René, 888
Viguera Franco, E. de, 690
Villeneuve, Anne de, 1394
Villot, Etienne C.E., 889
Vinogradov, Amal Rassam, 776, 777, 1331, 1332
Volpi, B., 1441

Waddy, Charles, 1056
Wahaib, Abdul Amir, 691
Wajihuddin, Ahmed, 692
Wakefield, F.M., 890
Wakim, Edward, 693
Wali, Abdel Gabber, 694
Wanner, L., 1057
Ward, Barbara E., 695
Wasfi, Atif Amin, 1058
Watson, A.D., 778
Watson, Hanan, 696
Webb, P.R.H., 428
Weisblat, A.M., 697
Wenig, Steffen, 1059
Wenner, M.W., 1614
Weil, Barbara, 1442
Weir, S., 1363
Westermarck, Edward, 1333
Westphal-Hellbusch, Sigrid, 698
White, Elizabeth, 326
Wigle, Laurel D., 1219
Wikan, Unni, 1341
Williams, Judith R., 1220
Williams, Neil Vincent, 1060
Wingate, R.O., 699
Winkel, Annegret, 1061

Women's International League for Peace and Freedom, 1222
Wood, Lucie A., 706
Woodsmall, R.F., 327, 707
Work, Margaret, 1064
World Student Christian Federation, 1594

El Yacoubi, R., 1335
Yafi, Abd, 328
Yammine, Randa, 709, 1223
Yankey, D., 1224
Yasseen, Shahzanan, 710, 1088
Yassin, Anas Ibn Youssef, 1389
Yotte, Yannick, 1595
Young, Ian, 893
Youssef, Nadia, 329, 330, 331, 332, 711, 712, 713, 714, 715, 716

Zagouri, A., 1336
Zanati, Mahmoud, 717
El Zayyat, L., 718
El-Zeghari, Hassan, 1337
Zeltzer, Moshe, 61
Zenkovsky, Sophie, 1445
Zerdoumi, N., 894, 895
Zghal, Abdel Kader, 1596, 1597
Ziadé, M., 1065
Zikria, Nizar, 333
Zu'bi, E., 1365
Zurayk, Huda C., 719, 1225
Zwemer, Samuel, 322, 323, 334

Subject Index

References are to entry numbers and not to pages.

Adult education *see* Education

Bedouins, 394, 563, 566, 723, 730, 737, 739, 761, 778, 802, 807, 823, 832, 834–837, 845, 851, 858, 888–890, 924, 1118, 1343, 1356, 1369, 1374, 1375, 1377, 1402, 1415, 1420
Bible, (women in the), 530, 531, 552, 554, 570
Biography, 217, 321, 960, 1116, 1119, 1122, 1151, 1366
Birth control, *see* Family planning
Birth order, 633–636, 1210

Circumcision, 476, 727, 745, 752, 760, 763, 779, 780, 781, 966, 1391, 1392, 1394, 1401, 1414, 1428, 1432, 1442
Clitoridectomy, *see* Circumcision

Development, (women in), 78, 82, 92, 96, 335, 337, 369, 372, 373, 384, 386, 387, 388, 414, 430, 431, 435, 437, 442, 457, 467, 490, 513, 522, 539, 544, 546, 573, 599, 612, 625, 632, 650, 658, 659, 660, 663, 664, 665, 671, 672, 673, 674, 675, 676, 686, 694, 703, 704, 750, 754, 772, 773, 774, 955, 1026, 1079, 1081, 1114, 1173, 1214, 1395, 1423, 1434, 1447, 1511, 1531, 1562, 1588, 1615
Divorce, 107, 126, 127, 129, 130, 163, 170, 182, 185, 221, 223, 281, 287, 289, 313, 724, 738, 741, 831, 839, 847, 855, 874–877, 941, 1090, 1192, 1205, 1290, 1297, 1336, 1476, 1479, 1486, 1509, 1524, 1547

Education, 50, 67, 69, 79, 329, 346, 347, 376, 397, 404, 425, 471, 492, 495, 510, 540, 546, 556, 557, 561, 591, 592, 593, 602, 603, 604, 623, 639, 640, 644, 646, 647, 648, 649, 652, 653, 656, 688, 689, 691, 701, 755, 766, 770, 771, 791, 846, 878, 897, 912, 916, 920, 943, 975, 988, 989, 995, 998, 1027, 1038, 1043, 1062, 1068, 1084, 1088, 1098, 1099, 1121, 1123, 1127, 1128, 1132, 1133, 1160, 1201, 1208, 1212, 1213, 1229, 1371, 1399, 1416, 1422, 1424, 1426, 1427, 1433, 1451, 1465, 1469, 1514, 1541, 1545, 1549,

Education *cont.*
  1554, 1559, 1567, 1575, 1576,
  1586, 1590, 1592, 1594, 1611,
  1615
Emancipation, *see* Rights of
  women
Employment, 69, 101, 330, 367,
  392, 434, 454, 485, 486, 487,
  501, 514, 518, 520, 648, 670,
  677, 678, 712, 713, 714, 716,
  785, 790, 792, 793, 854, 857,
  891, 946, 958, 963, 1002, 1003,
  1060, 1095, 1101, 1106, 1112,
  1124, 1129, 1132, 1137, 1141,
  1148, 1160, 1161, 1203, 1209,
  1212, 1213, 1236, 1280, 1286,
  1287, 1301, 1305, 1306, 1315,
  1316, 1337, 1416, 1418, 1419,
  1425, 1431, 1440, 1444, 1452,
  1453, 1454, 1463, 1467, 1475,
  1516, 1517, 1519, 1526, 1534,
  1535, 1536, 1538, 1539, 1542,
  1584
Endogamy, *see* Marriage
Equality, 267, 291, 475, 477, 950,
  1019, 1046, 1197, 1413, 1503
Exogamy, *see* Marriage

Family, 12, 15, 17, 21, 23, 32, 33,
  36, 39, 41, 42, 46, 54, 55, 71,
  98, 106, 119, 161, 164, 191,
  211, 218, 224, 233, 245, 266,
  271, 284, 351, 497, 558, 638,
  711, 728, 813, 909, 948, 962,
  969, 974, 983, 1000, 1011,
  1058, 1060, 1077, 1089, 1156,
  1166, 1167, 1174, 1184, 1239,
  1241, 1242, 1250, 1258, 1287,
  1291, 1292, 1317, 1337, 1383,
  1393, 1461, 1473, 1477, 1478,
  1498, 1499, 1508, 1543, 1578
Family Planning, 31, 64, 65, 102,
  379, 942, 971, 973, 979, 1078,
  1109, 1152, 1294, 1295, 1296,
  1335, 1513
Fertility, 122, 330, 519, 609, 715,
  927, 929, 979, 994, 1098, 1109,
  1224, 1225, 1256, 1472

Harem, 382, 409, 579, 590, 769,
  922, 1022, 1579, 1605
Health, 102a, 381, 775, 893, 925,
  961, 965, 1028, 1040, 1153,
  1176, 1215, 1216, 1303, 1344,
  1352, 1399, 1419, 1435, 1466,
  1604, 1606

Infibulation, *see* Circumcision
International Women's Year, 83,
  138, 371, 651, 679, 680, 705,
  944, 977, 1075, 1130, 1346,
  1364, 1390, 1448
Islam, (Women in,) 99, 100, 103,
  104, 105, 113, 115, 118, 123,
  124, 134, 136, 137, 138, 140,
  141, 142, 143, 144, 145, 146,
  148, 179, 181, 186, 188, 189,
  193, 198, 199, 201, 202, 203,
  204, 205, 206, 207, 208, 214,
  216, 219, 225, 226, 229, 230,
  232, 236, 247, 250, 254, 258,
  277, 282, 284, 292, 293, 296,
  297, 298, 299, 308, 333, 445,
  526, 805, 860, 861, 871, 923,
  1057, 1304, 1450, 1500, 1596
Islamic law, 117, 128, 132, 150,
  156, 157, 158, 160, 165, 172,
  180, 183, 191, 209, 212, 213,
  224, 231, 234, 246, 249, 288,
  301

Koran (women in the), 108, 118,
  133, 139, 147, 173, 176, 253,
  305, 309

Laws and legal status, 63, 89,
  117, 120, 121, 122, 134, 136,
  137, 237, 249, 264, 280, 295,
  299, 301, 317, 318, 338, 352,
  355, 357, 358, 359, 368, 399,
  429, 431, 432, 439, 441, 443,
  594, 597, 598, 669, 691, 710,
  777, 879, 881, 902, 910, 929,
  934, 944, 959, 974, 977, 979,
  982, 999, 1041, 1048, 1049,
  1051, 1080, 1126, 1134, 1143,
  1149, 1163, 1190, 1194, 1233,

1243, 1300, 1315, 1345, 1365,
1367, 1380, 1396, 1409, 1412,
1429, 1443, 1464, 1467, 1483,
1546, 1553, 1568, 1569, 1572,
1587, 1599, 1616
Literature (women in), 214, 341,
342, 343, 344, 345, 350, 390,
396, 398, 456, 460, 461, 524,
529, 532, 560, 574, 583, 643,
720, 721, 758, 843, 1044, 1143,
1523

Marriage, 107, 109, 111, 114,
116, 125, 135, 165, 168, 169,
177, 182, 183, 187, 194, 200,
220, 221, 222, 227, 228, 238,
241, 242, 243, 257, 269, 272,
279, 300, 302, 303, 312, 314,
365, 366, 374, 403, 405, 411,
412, 417, 428, 462, 465, 474,
500, 511, 515, 516, 534, 571,
575, 577, 586, 616, 619, 631,
706, 732, 735, 743, 764, 767,
786, 803, 809, 818, 825, 833,
863, 870, 873, 874, 875, 876,
877, 882, 884, 885, 886, 908,
913, 924, 940, 948, 954, 976,
1020, 1069, 1091, 1117, 1136,
1145, 1147, 1226, 1231, 1238,
1245, 1251, 1254, 1257, 1261,
1267, 1284, 1290, 1333, 1351,
1360, 1363, 1387, 1393, 1404,
1415, 1439, 1445, 1449, 1470,
1474, 1480, 1492, 1501, 1502,
1521, 1544, 1552, 1555, 1556,
1557, 1558, 1570, 1591, 1602,
1603, 1612
Maternity, *see* Mothers
Middle East—social conditions,
1, 2, 5–10, 13, 14, 16, 18, 19,
24, 26–30, 34, 35, 38, 40, 44,
45, 47–49, 51–53. *See also*
pages 23–27.
Mothers, 547, 622, 690, 757, 762,
856, 907, 1017, 1083, 1155,
1191, 1195, 1200, 1286, 1296,
1302, 1350, 1595

Nomads, *see* Bedouins

Politics (women in), 331, 413,
427, 448, 449, 450, 564, 567,
657, 682, 751, 796, 828, 829,
844, 930, 1029, 1135, 1157,
1194, 1219, 1221, 1223, 1313,
1342, 1362, 1407, 1408, 1411,
1421, 1589
Polygamy, *see* Marriage
Purdah, 256, 274, 275, 276, 286,
326, 409

Relations between the sexes, *see*
Sex
Rights of women, 25, 74, 116,
133, 159, 167, 171, 174, 178,
192, 196, 197, 209, 210, 211,
213, 239, 252, 254, 316, 391,
451, 562, 565, 784, 840, 864,
894, 898, 915, 919, 938, 980,
1015, 1021, 1034, 1035, 1037,
1111, 1230, 1260, 1281, 1285,
1305, 1329, 1385, 1406, 1410,
1458, 1462, 1488, 1515, 1533,
1583, 1610
Rural conditions, 2, 3, 37, 46, 78,
332, 340, 349, 364, 373, 385,
395, 414, 422, 457, 467, 539,
559, 573, 589, 610, 628, 697,
708, 742, 754, 895, 900, 901,
904, 905, 914, 952, 967, 1018,
1025, 1064, 1073, 1074, 1103,
1164, 1196, 1199, 1206, 1207,
1211, 1214, 1220, 1242, 1243,
1244, 1259, 1262, 1263, 1264,
1271, 1288, 1298, 1311, 1321,
1331, 1332, 1348, 1374, 1395,
1422, 1461, 1578, 1609

Segregation of sexes, *see* Sex
Sex, 36, 152, 153, 154, 155, 195,
240, 290, 470, 536, 543, 581,
582, 600, 611, 629, 698, 776,
797, 925, 986, 987, 1231, 1234,
1244, 1265, 1274, 1306, 1307,
1320, 1322, 1341, 1355, 1356,
1503, 1506, 1522

Sex roles, *see* Sex
Social role, 20, 21, 78, 81, 82, 87, 88, 91, 92, 190, 251, 283, 294, 319, 336, 337, 356, 385, 402, 423, 446, 480, 491, 495, 512, 565, 606, 614, 617, 719, 830, 932, 939, 947, 972, 1005, 1053, 1100, 1105, 1110, 1113, 1131, 1178, 1400, 1403, 1405, 1423, 1434, 1437, 1468, 1472, 1490, 1499, 1504, 1527, 1534, 1568, 1596, 1613
Societies and clubs, 76, 77, 97, 447, 453, 466, 484, 548, 572, 683, 815, 918, 1004, 1016, 1038, 1052, 1094, 1096, 1097, 1125, 1177, 1339, 1349, 1353, 1358, 1384, 1421, 1436, 1438, 1441, 1446, 1459, 1460, 1528, 1600
Statutes, 117, 131, 150, 156, 261, 264, 299, 434, 441, 744, 800, 937, 948, 951, 1067, 1089, 1092, 1150, 1250, 1266, 1397, 1485, 1487, 1494, 1560, 1565, 1570, 1571

Touaregs, *see* Bedouins

Veil, 263, 278, 320, 324, 393, 421, 499, 525, 535, 555, 613, 630, 700, 845, 852, 901, 1009, 1328, 1330, 1386, 1455, 1493
Vocational education, *see* Education